THE COMPLETE
HOME GUIDE TO
FURNITURE FINISHING
AND REFINISHING

Bernard Gladstone

ILLUSTRATED BY ROBERT STRIMBAN

A FIRESIDE BOOK PUBLISHED BY SIMON AND SCHUSTER • NEW YORK

COPYRIGHT © 1981 BY BERNARD GLADSTONE
ALL RIGHTS RESERVED
INCLUDING THE RIGHT OF REPRODUCTION
IN WHOLE OR IN PART IN ANY FORM
PUBLISHED BY SIMON AND SCHUSTER
A DIVISION OF GULF & WESTERN CORPORATION
SIMON & SCHUSTER BUILDING
ROCKEFELLER CENTER
1230 AVENUE OF THE AMERICAS
NEW YORK, NEW YORK 10020
SIMON AND SCHUSTER AND COLOPHON ARE TRADEMARKS OF SIMON & SCHUSTER
FIRESIDE AND COLOPHON ARE TRADEMARKS OF SIMON & SCHUSTER

MANUFACTURED IN THE UNITED STATES OF AMERICA

10 9 8 7 6 5 4 3 2 1
10 9 8 7 6 5 4 3 2 1 Pbk.
LIBRARY OF CONGRESS CATALOGING IN PUBLICATION DATA

GLADSTONE, BERNARD.
    THE COMPLETE GUIDE TO FURNITURE FINISHING AND
REFINISHING.

    (A FIRESIDE BOOK)
    INCLUDES INDEX.
    1. FURNITURE FINISHING. I. TITLE.
TT199.4.G54   684.1'043   81-1029
                                AACR2

ISBN 0-671-25603-3
    0-671-25604-1 Pbk.

CONTENTS

CONTENTS

Introduction

Most people stand in awe of the "old way" of doing things—particularly when they gaze at a piece of fine old furniture and think about the "old-time" craftsmen who used to patiently apply those beautiful wood finishes. What countless hours of laborious sanding, hand rubbing, and polishing had to go into their work!

The idea of spending all that time and hard labor on furniture finishing has, unfortunately, discouraged many would-be home furniture finishers from tackling jobs that they might otherwise be tempted to try. Yet such drudgery is largely no longer necessary.

Regardless of whether you want to finish an inexpensive piece of unpainted pine furniture or refinish an old relic that has long been consigned to the attic, modern, easy-to-use materials and simplified working techniques make it possible for you to do a thoroughly professional job. The new finishes are not only simpler to apply, they also last longer and are easier to maintain.

Of course, it would be foolish for an inexperienced amateur to start out by trying to refinish a valuable piece of antique furniture or an expensive heirloom, but such restrictions aside, anyone can learn—with a little patience—to apply a fine finish on almost any type of furniture.

The detailed, nontechnical instructions in this book will tell you not only how to achieve a handsome, durable finish, but also how to apply various specialized finishes that will enable you to rejuvenate old pieces and give them a personal touch. With only a little experience you will soon find that furniture finishing is one of the most rewarding do-it-yourself projects you can tackle. Think of the satisfaction you'll get from turning an "ugly duckling" into a "beautiful swan." You will also be rewarded by substantial savings because of the high cost of having pieces refinished professionally.

INTRODUCTION

All this is possible because of the new and greatly improved finishing materials now widely available, which our forefathers never knew about. They had to work with the best materials available at that time—but this does not mean that these are still the best. This book explains how to select and apply the new finishes and points out how to use them for the effect you want under varying conditions.

Where "old-time" methods are still useful, or where they are still the only way to get certain finishes, I have included them. But wherever there is a quicker and easier way to achieve the same look and quality without a lot of hard work, then I have described the newer methods and materials.

For example, years ago when a finisher wanted a low-gloss or "rubbed" effect, he first had to build up a finish with many coats of slow-drying, high-gloss varnish. This had to harden for a week or so, then it was rubbed and rubbed with successively milder abrasives until the finish was dulled to the desired sheen. Nowadays anyone can get the same effect with modern, low-luster varnishes that dry to a flat, satin, or semi-gloss finish—all with little or no rubbing, and in a fraction of the time.

These varnishes, as well as most of the other finishing materials mentioned in this book, are widely available in most local paint and hardware stores. However, when specialized or hard-to-find materials are the only way to achieve a specific finish, or when you prefer one of these for whatever reason, then I also included methods for these materials. You can order what you need from supply houses that sell to professional furniture finishers, or from mail-order companies that cater to home craftsmen.

All material in this book is cross-referenced where necessary to avoid repetition, and to help you locate answers to related problems. There is also a complete index at the back for a detailed listing of specific subjects. At any rate, I strongly advise you to study the table of contents before starting your first project to help you understand how the material in this book is organized, and to learn where to find information on the various finishing methods. I think you're going to be pleasantly surprised to find home finishing much less work and considerably more fun than you had thought!

1 · Decisions, Decisions: Choosing the Right Finish

FOR EVERY PIECE OF FURNITURE, there's a finish, and one that will please you, the finisher, as well. Nothing will be as important to the success of your project as this first decision about which finish you should use.

When you speak of a "finish" specifically, you should know that you're actually talking about the product that seals and protects the wood from heat, dryness, moisture—anything that can mar and destroy it. You're not talking about the actual wood itself—color or feel, for example—nor are you talking about staining, repairing, or stripping—although all are part of refinishing and will certainly make a difference in how you apply a new finish or restore an old one.

There are many good methods and materials to choose from, but to make an intelligent, painless decision, you have to see what's available and learn how to match it up with the style of your piece, its condition, and the amount of time and effort you want to spend on it. With the right information, in fact, you may not have to do any refinishing at all.

RESTORATION VS. REFINISHING

You've found the piece and you love it. In fact, you'd love it just the way it is, if only the finish weren't so dingy, and it weren't scratched, watermarked, and kind of dented here and there. Your refinishing plans are to make it look just the way it did when it was new.

Don't refinish—yet. When a piece is in the condition just described, it often doesn't need a total refinishing job. Turn first to Chapter 7, "Restoration: When You'd Like It Just the Way It Is, If Only . . ." on page 104. Could be you'll have a lot less to do than you thought, and you will be surprised at the kind of restoration work possible.

MATCHING STYLE TO FINISH

Whatever the style of your piece, or its condition, you'll be choosing from basically three types of finishes: a transparent finish, which allows all of the wood, grain, color, etc., to show through; a translucent finish, which allows much of the wood to show through, particularly grain, but can change the color and obscure the less than perfect characteristics; and an opaque finish, such as paint, which covers everything—often very interestingly.

Generally, the finer, more formal, and more traditional the piece, the more likely it is to call for a natural wood finish. Transparent or translucent? That depends on the beauty and the color of the wood. No gloss or high gloss? It's a matter of taste, but satin luster to high gloss is traditional, and you can get a satin finish without too much work.

Don't judge the wood on color alone. Grain is frequently more important. You can lighten a too-dark piece or stain a too-light one, and bring out the beauty of the grain as well.

Actually, it's probably the wood that's most likely to influence your choice of a finish. Lots of modern pieces are made of beautiful woods you wouldn't cover. You might choose to finish them with a no-gloss, "natural" sealer for a less formal effect. You might even choose a "natural" for a traditional piece to blend it with the casual mixture of styles and colors in your home.

If you have a piece made of inexpensive or uninteresting wood, but it's a wood finish you want, you may be able to use one of the translucent stains and finishes. The same goes for a piece made of many different woods. However, such pieces were often made to be painted, and you can improve even the most uninteresting piece with an easy and interesting lacquer-like enamel or "antiquing" job. The same goes for some old, battered pieces that are sound and serviceable, but not so naturally beautiful, no matter what their wood or their condition. The opaque finishes can be very beautiful, and shouldn't be ignored even for some better pieces.

Of course, you might not be able to tell what kind of wood you have if it's hiding under an old, murky finish or layers of paint. You can strip a small section to determine the wood, and then see if there's an easier alternative to stripping the entire piece, because getting down to bare wood can be lots of work.

THE CONDITION OF THE PIECE AND HOW TO CURE IT

For making finishing decisions, it's the condition of the wood that's most important. But if your piece is falling apart, do turn to Chapter 3, page 30, first. Chapter 3 will tell you how to treat gouges, scratches, holes, and the other defects that can show up on the surface of an otherwise fine piece. You can patch them, you can even dye your patches to match your wood, and depending on how few and small your patches are, you may even be able to get away with a transparent or translucent finish. But patches are never quite invisible, and for the really battered piece, no matter how fine, opaque finishing may be the only answer.

One advantage of an opaque finish is that you don't need to match up the patches, because they're going to be covered, and this means less work. If your piece is really battered, try antiquing it, or giving it a good "fake" wood finish, and/or a touch of gilt—but be careful about opaquing a real antique as you could be really lowering its value.

By the way, you might consider a tough old finish on your piece a part of its "condition," especially if it's going to take lots of work to get it off—so much work it may not be worth it.

THE FUNCTION IS THE FINISH

For every function, there is a finish—and in every variation you can think of. Want a glossy "piano-type" finish on your heirloom dining-room table that has to take as many spills as any Formica surface? You can do it with polyurethane —the toughest finish in clear or opaque.

For children's furniture, you might want to use a colored enamel with a polyurethane base. It is no tougher than the clear version, and nothing is completely marproof, but you can repair an enamel finish a lot easier than the "piano" variety. Besides, kids like color. They haven't yet learned that wood is sacred. And don't forget the antique finish for a more traditional look. It has an enamel base, and actually looks good with dents.

Most of the new finishes are tougher than their old counterparts, and you'll find them easy to use—both in finishing and around the house. And there are not-so-tough but beautiful finishes, for gentler handling.

MARRYING THE WORK TO THE WORKER

Now we get down to the know-thyself part, and the know-thy-piece as well. You're going to have to measure how much time you have to give—or how much time you *want* to give—to this project.

The thing to remember is that most clear or natural wood finishes require more preparation than opaque finishes do. They may be no harder to lay on, but they almost always require stripping—a step you can eliminate with opaque paints. There may be more patching to do, and they're likely to require staining as well.

Time and labor are not the only considerations. Your decision should also depend on what you really like, the effect you want your piece to have, and how much the piece is worth to you in any state of finish. To opt for a finish because it's easy to apply and then wind up hating it is a total waste of time. Getting what you want, no matter how long it takes, may be worth it. Or maybe there's an interesting compromise. You're bound to find it as we go into more detail about the steps leading to, and the final laying on of, the finishes.

2 · Unfinishing Furniture—Or How to Be a Sensational Stripper

STRIPPING IS THE BIG DEAL of the refinishing business. See a nice piece that's been brought down to beautifully bared wood at a country auction, and you'll also find an auctioneer exhorting bidders to spend more for that very reason. Often, they will.

The same goes for city auctions and even some antique dealers. The proprietor will unhesitatingly admit that part of the elevated price tag is for having undone the mistakes of the ages.

We're not talking about stripping historically interesting finishes, just someone's whim to turn Grandma's great dining chairs into porch furniture with layers of paint, or the like. But, say professionals, it's the undoing of mistakes and the unfinishing of neglected and damaged surfaces that is likely to make the most mess.

Please note, the words are "most mess," not "most difficult," though stripping is the one area of refinishing that may call for a bit more muscle and patience than the rest.

But whatever method you use, you will save a lot of money and, most important, have a great deal of control over the quality and quantity of unfinishing if you do it yourself, and that does figure greatly in the beauty of the finished piece.

Basically, there are two methods of stripping. You can strip mechanically—by sanding and scraping—or chemically—with commercial, readily available paint and varnish removers.

SANDING FOR LESS MESS AND VERY LITTLE MONEY

The amount of sandpaper needed to strip a piece costs far less than an equivalent amount of chemical remover. It also makes less of a mess. It's easier to vacuum up sawdust-type residue than it is to protect an area from the spills, drips, and general mess chemical removers are sometimes prone to create.

Still, cheap and neat notwithstanding, sanding as a removal procedure is in disrepute among many professionals, especially those who handle furniture that is old, or delicately cut, or heavily carved or turned. On these kinds of pieces, the drawbacks of sanding can be considerable.

The wood on old furniture, for example, darkens a certain way with age, and acquires a special appearance or "feel" that is the result of years of being touched, polished, etc. It's what's known as the "patina," and it's nigh onto impossible to duplicate. With the kind of sanding required to strip a piece, a thin layer of wood usually disappears with the finish, and it's goodbye patina.

It's possible, of course, to sand with a very fine abrasive and a gentle hand. It's done all the time between coats of finish, or as the last step before a finish goes on, as you'll find out in the next chapter. But removing a finish calls for a heavier paper and a heavier hand—heavy enough, say experts, to mar carving or even change the shape of a delicately cut leg. Even on plain pieces, you have to be careful not to round corners. But once you're forewarned, the chances of destroying sharp edges are greatly reduced. And despite some pros' edicts that sanding has no place in the "unfinishing" process, there are times when it is the most practical, and sometimes only way to go.

Sanding is most effective on flat surfaces, so if you've got a relatively uninteresting chest, say, that's not old enough to have a patina, and it's covered by some tough old paint, sanding may just be the fastest and easiest way to get it off. The same goes for a table with plain legs, one that only your refinishing will make beautiful. Or you may have an old piece with a finish so badly scarred, stained, gouged, or otherwise damaged that the only answer—if you're hell-bent on a natural wood finish—may be to get down below the surface to new wood.

It is possible to give wood a more aged look—even the raw, new stuff. That's what staining and refinishing can do, and you'll learn how in later chapters, so don't be afraid to get down to the bare wood—*if you have to*. Many times, you will have to sand even after the finish has been removed chemically. As you grow more experienced, you'll begin to get a feel for when sanding's most appropriate, and which grade of sandpaper and tools to use.

By the way, we are talking about hand sanding at this point. There are sanding machines that can make the work go very quickly, but these have to be used with care, and it won't pay you to buy one if you're only stripping a single piece.

Although most of us refer to all abrasive papers as "sandpaper," they don't really have sand on them. The oldest type is flint paper, which is coated with grains of quartz, a natural mineral that looks very much like sand. It's also the cheapest of all abrasive papers, but it dulls quickly, clogs easily, and wears out much more rapidly than other types. Ultimately it costs no less than the newer and better types which are coated with synthetic minerals.

The most versatile and most widely available type of flexible abrasive is aluminum oxide paper (also called production paper). Aluminum oxide is a synthetic mineral that is much harder, sharper, and longer-lasting than flint or quartz in normal use. In addition, aluminum oxide papers have a stronger, more tear-resistant backing than flint papers.

Garnet paper is not quite so hard or long-wearing as aluminum oxide, but many finishers prefer it because it works particularly well on raw wood. I personally have never discovered why, but you might want to try it sometime. You might see something I don't.

Sandpapers are also graded according to the size of the abrasive particles coating them. The lower the number, the coarser the grade—30 is very coarse and will leave deep scratches, while 600 is very fine, and is mainly used for polishing. Sometimes papers are simply marked Very Coarse, Coarse, Medium, Fine, etc., or simply M for medium, F for fine, and so on.

For stripping purposes, 80 is best. It's somewhere between coarse and medium, and is rough enough to take off the finish without taking a lot of wood with it.

All sanding on flat surfaces, from rough to fine, is usually done better with a sanding block. You can apply more pressure without tearing the paper or having it clog unevenly, and it helps you to apply pressure more evenly so you're not sanding down one part more than another.

You can buy commercially made sanding blocks or wedges, padded with foam rubber or felt, in different sizes and shapes and at a pretty reasonable price in most paint and hardware stores. Most experienced finishers, however, prefer to make their own. They simply cut blocks of wood to the desired size and shape, then cover the working face with thick felt, foam, or sponge rubber.

Sanding blocks can be made in any convenient shape or size. For best results, blocks should have face lined with felt or rubber.

Don't ignore the padding. A block without any resilient material between it and the paper can cause deep scratches—especially if the paper tears or if a large particle of abrasive grit gets caught between the block and the surface being sanded.

For sanding areas where a block is not convenient, tear a standard sheet of sandpaper in half, then fold each piece in half with the abrasive sides facing out. You can now hold each of these folded sheets comfortably in the palm of your hand and work with the double thickness. When one side becomes dull or clogged, simply flip the folded sheet over to expose the other side. The reason you tear the sheet in half before you fold it—instead of folding the large sheet four ways—is to keep the abrasive faces from rubbing against each other. This would only shorten their life by causing them to dull prematurely.

Sand with the grain. Any small specks of finish left can be scraped off with a very gentle sideswipe with the paper against the grain—or you might try scrap-

For convenient hand sanding, tear a sheet of sandpaper in half and fold each piece in half, with abrasive sides facing out.

ing it off, again gently, with a piece of glass held edgewise at right angles to the surface so it won't cut into the wood. Any scratches incurred during this process can be smoothed later.

Of course, your sanding will go even faster, and will take much less effort, if you use a sanding machine. And if you really get into finishing, a sanding machine can be a good investment. You can use it for all kinds of sanding jobs, especially in the final stages of smoothing the wood when flat surfaces are involved.

Best for this kind of job are the orbital or belt sanders. Forget the disc sander. (See also "Special Tools for the Stripper," page 26.)

Orbital sanders are slower working than belt sanders, but belt sanders can be used efficiently only on fairly large, flat surfaces. Also, they cut so fast they will go right through the finish and start removing wood at a fearful clip if you're not careful.

With either type of machine, try to sand with the grain as much as possible to avoid leaving scratch marks. Again, start with 80 paper, then switch to progressively finer grits to remove scratches left by the coarser grades. For the intermediate sanding, use 100 or 120, then for the final smoothing, 220 (see "Sanding for Smoothness," page 43).

Aluminum oxide papers are probably the most widely used with electric sanders, because flint papers will not stand up under machine use.

If you run into places not easily reached with sandpaper—inside corners, for example, or around carvings—then you'll have to use steel wool or a scraper of some kind. A hook scraper is perfect for this. Steel wool cuts much slower than

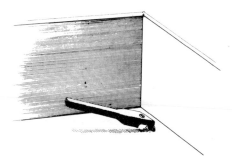

Hook scrapers are often the only way to get into corners and up against dividers where you cannot reach with sandpaper.

sandpaper does, so only the coarsest grades will be of any value in removing old finishes. However, it is easier to use on curved or carved surfaces, and it can be twisted into strands which you can use in shoeshine fashion around grooved spindles and carvings on turned legs. More about steel wool under "Tools for the Stripper," page 29.

Hook-type hand scrapers will enable you to reach into corners and cabinet interiors, but make sure the blade is sharp and straight—you don't want to gouge and scratch the surface.

CHEMICAL REMOVERS—THE BEGINNER'S BEST FRIEND

Chemical removers are, as I said earlier, more expensive than sandpaper—and they are messy. But lay down the newspapers, put on your oldest clothes, and open the windows—because it's all worth it. You may make a bigger mess than you're supposed to, you may use more remover than you have to, it may take longer to take the gunk off the first time around, but with removers you are less likely to make a mistake—especially one that will ruin delicate carvings or the patina.

Remember, when we talk about "finishes," what we're really talking about is the product that seals the wood itself—not the stain or the wood's color. And what chemical removers remove is finish—and little else. They're fairly failproof and can be the beginner's best friend. What's more, a wide variety of chemical removers are commonly available in paint and hardware stores. However, all work in basically the same way. They contain special solvents and chemicals that soften and "lift" or blister up old finish so it can easily be wiped, scraped, or washed away to expose bare wood.

Some removers are liquid and some are creamy or semi-paste in consistency. As a rule, the liquids cost less, but the thicker semi-paste types are better for most furniture stripping jobs. They "stay put," without running and dripping when used on vertical surfaces, and they don't evaporate or dry out as quickly. And a remover that stays wet longer keeps on working longer. The longer a remover stays wet and in contact with the old finish, the deeper and more thoroughly it will penetrate in a single application. Liquid removers often have to be reapplied several times to penetrate multi-layer finishes.

Another important difference between removers is their flammability. Many are highly inflammable and must be used with extreme caution when working indoors. Weather permitting, you should work outside or in the garage (with the door open). Others are nonflammable and cost only slightly more, so choose one of these when you must work indoors.

To keep paint removers from drying out or evaporating before they can completely penetrate and soften the old finish, manufacturers usually add special ingredients that retard evaporation by floating to the surface and keeping air out. In many removers, this is a waxlike compound which leaves a residue that must be neutralized or washed away when the job is done. Otherwise a new finish will not adhere properly. However, many of the newer removers use a retardant that contains no wax, and these supposedly need no washing with solvent. Usually labeled as "no-wash" or "self-neutralizing," these removers come in both liquid and semi-paste forms, and they create less problems than those that contain wax. Nevertheless, it is best with either type to play safe and wipe the surface down with paint thinner or denatured alcohol after using the remover.

If you do decide to use the type that requires an after-rinse, make sure you do a thorough job of rinsing—especially in corners and inside carvings where it's easy to miss small bits of residue. Areas that have not been rinsed clean with solvent may not be noticeable when the wood is bare, but after the first one or two coats of finish have been applied you may find, to your dismay, that the new finish will start bubbling up in those spots where some of the old remover was not thoroughly washed off.

One of the easiest types of varnish remover you can use is a water-wash type. Most widely available in semi-paste form, it is also usually nonflammable. The advantage of using this remover is that after the old finish has been thoroughly softened with a heavy application, you can wash everything off by simply scrubbing with a brush or a piece of steel wool dipped in water. You can even take the piece outside and hose it down with water, while you scrub the finish off with a stiff brush. But you do have to be careful about using water on old pieces of furniture. Many of them are assembled with old-fashioned glue that is not water-resistant. And *never* use water on a piece of furniture that is covered with veneer. The surface will almost always wrinkle or loosen, destroying the veneer.

To minimize the mess, if possible take the piece outdoors or out to the garage or down to the basement to do your work. If you must work in the house, cover the floor and nearby areas to protect them. But don't depend on plastic dropcloths. Many chemical removers dissolve plastic. Put a few layers of old newspaper down, or use an old bedsheet or blanket covered with several layers of newspaper. Wear rubber gloves to protect your hands, and if you will be working on surfaces above eye level, wear goggles to protect your eyes.

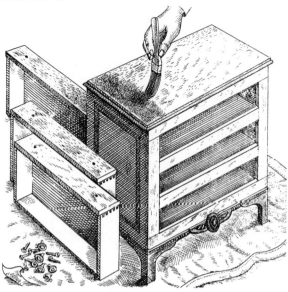

To prepare for chemical stripping, remove hardware and position the parts of the piece, such as bureau drawers, so that the surfaces to be stripped are horizontal. The bureau case can, of course, be tipped on its side or back when stripping sides and front.

Before starting to apply the remover, take off knobs, hinges, handles, and all other hardware. Stand the drawers up so the fronts are horizontal, and lay doors flat after the hinges have been removed.

Some repairs are done after stripping, and some before. Now is the time to look for loose joints. If there are many that need repair, take them apart before stripping. You may simply want to strip now, and wait to make repairs, or you may want to repair them before working with the remover. Either is possible, and to make the best choice, turn to Chapter 3, "Preparing for the New Finish —or What to Fix First," and read the first two sections, "Gluing and Other Nailless Methods of Mending" and "Hiding Nails and Screws When You Have to Use Them." It'll just take a few minutes, and you'll know how to proceed. You'll get to that glorious remover gunk soon enough.

The easiest way to apply the remover is with an old paintbrush, or with an inexpensive brush that you can throw away afterward. Lay the remover on in thick layers with a minimum of back-and-forth brushing so that you don't disturb the film any more than necessary as you apply it.

Too much brushing only slows up the chemical action, because it allows air to enter the solution and speeds evaporation of the solvent. If you are working outdoors, avoid working in direct sunlight, since this too hastens evaporation and shortens the working time.

As a rule, it is best to concentrate on one side or section at a time. Apply the remover to the area in a heavy layer, then wait about 15 to 20 minutes and test one corner with a putty knife to see if the old finish is softened all the way down to the bare wood. Ideally, all layers of finish should come off down to the bare wood with a single scraping. If your test indicates that the finish is not soft all the way down, and if the remover is still wet (and therefore still working), wait another 5 or 10 minutes and try again. If the remover has still not softened the finish all the way down to the raw wood, stop scraping and apply

Lay remover on in thick layers, using the flat side of the brush more than its tip.

Softened finish should come off down to the raw wood with one scraping. If not, put more remover on and allow a longer working time.

a second coat of the remover right on top of the original one. Allow this to work for another 10 or 15 minutes and then try again. Whatever you do, don't skimp on remover, and don't wait longer than about 20 minutes before scraping off everything that you've put on thus far. It's too hard to scrape off otherwise.

By the way, you may remember back in Chapter 1, we spoke about testing pieces that have an opaque finish to see what the wood is like underneath. This is the way to do it, at least if you're a beginner. The expert may be able to tell much more from a small scrape. But most of us have to see a reasonable expanse of wood—at least 6 inches—to tell if we have anything worth stripping. It's worth the few extra dollars and half an hour to find out.

On flat surfaces a putty knife is probably the quickest and easiest way to scrape most of the softened material off. In grooves or crevices, or where there are many carvings, you'll really appreciate the advantages of using a water-wash remover. All you do is dip a stiff-bristled brush into water or a detergent solution, and then simply scrub the softened residue out.

If you're not using a water-wash remover, you can accomplish the same thing with coarse steel wool, a wire brush, or a scrub brush dipped into paint thinner. Again, read the label on your product carefully, and know what you're buying. Then you'll best know the most effective way to scrub up.

After the entire surface has been scraped clean, look over the piece carefully

When using a water-wash remover, softened paint or varnish can be scrubbed off with a stiff brush dipped into water, without need for scraping.

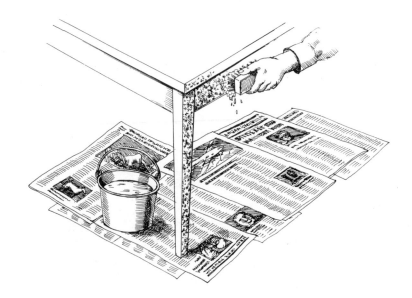

to make sure there are no spots where small patches of the old finish are still visible. Often these will show up as dark spots, or as "glazed" spots which are still slightly glossy. Although barely noticeable on the raw wood, these will really stand out after the new finish is applied, especially if the refinishing process requires a penetrating type of wood stain. In those spots, the stain will not soak in as much as it does on the rest of the wood—if at all. To prevent this, recoat the missed spots with remover and then scrub with steel wool.

When the wood has been stripped clean allow it to dry thoroughly, then sand lightly with 220 sandpaper. This not only gives the wood a final smoothing, it also removes any film or chemicals that may still be left on the surface, and helps to open the pores of the wood so that the new finish will penetrate properly.

A WORD ABOUT DIP-AND-STRIP SERVICES

The problem with using one of these services is threefold. First, if the person doing the work isn't careful, you'll lose not only the old finish, but that patina you sought to save by refusing to sand. In fact, by this method, you almost always do lose the patina. Second, wood fibers are likely to be damaged or so dried out by being left too long in the bath that you'll have to sand anyway. It happens very frequently to the same pros who condemn sanding. Third, these companies tend to charge a lot, which might be all right if the caustic remover used didn't often "burn" your wood darker. And we haven't even gotten to the tales of furniture coming apart at the joints—although in all fairness, this rarely happens these days.

USING BLEACHES TO LIGHTEN WOOD

As mentioned earlier, paint and varnish removers take off finish—not stain, or at least not very much of it. So if you are working on a pine or maple piece, say, that has been stained to look like walnut or mahogany, and you want to bring it back to oak, you may be able to do it with bleach. Or maybe you are hoping to get down to light wood so you can restain to match the rest of the furniture in the living room.

Whatever your reason, if, after stripping, you find the wood not light enough to suit you, don't despair. Bleach is not only capable of lightening wood all over, it can be very effective in removing blemishes and discolored areas that have penetrated too deeply into the wood to be removed by sanding.

There are three types of bleach you can use on furniture: liquid laundry bleach which has a chlorinated base; oxalic acid; or one of the two-solution wood bleaches that are specifically sold for this purpose. All are effective only on bare wood, so all the old finish must be taken off before bleaching—and there must be no skips or missed spots or the bleach will not soak in and you will wind up with a blotchy, uneven job.

For the same reason, it's important that close-grained woods, such as maple, be thoroughly sanded to open the wood's pores before bleaching. Otherwise, an uneven job.

Of the three bleaches mentioned, laundry bleach is the weakest and the hardest to control. However, applying it several times is often convenient when you don't want to bleach an entire piece but just lighten some discolored areas. It's also good for taking out ink spots or watermarks that have darkened the wood in places.

Oxalic acid, to my mind, is the most useful of all wood bleaches. It's stronger and easier to control than commercially mixed laundry bleaches, and comes in non-spillable crystal form. To use, dissolve as many crystals as you can in a container of hot (hot is important) water. Mop this solution on over the piece while it's still hot, then allow the bleach to dry. Rinse off with plenty of clear water. Repeat the treatment if you want the wood even lighter.

If you're still not satisfied, try strengthening the action by combining oxalic acid with hyposulfite—ordinary photographer's hypo, available in any camera store. Apply the oxalic acid first. As it begins to dry, mop on the hypo solution (3 ounces of hypo in 1 quart of warm water). Let sit for about 15 to 20 minutes, then rinse off with plenty of clean water.

If even this is not light enough then there is still another double-barreled solution—the two-solution chemical wood bleaches.

These are the most expensive of the bleaches, but they're also the strongest, the most effective, and probably the fastest-acting. You spread one solution on the piece first, then follow up with the second.

Pour the first solution into a plastic or glass bowl (not metal). Then take a synthetic nylon brush or rubber sponge, dip it into the solution, and spread the solution on the surface of your piece.

Allow the first solution to remain on the piece for the length of time recommended on the label or in the directions, usually 10 to 20 minutes. Then apply the second solution in much the same way. Again, let stand for the recommended amount of time, but this time, keep your eye on the wood. If it looks as if it is getting lighter than you want it to, you can stop the action at any time by flooding the surface with ordinary household vinegar.

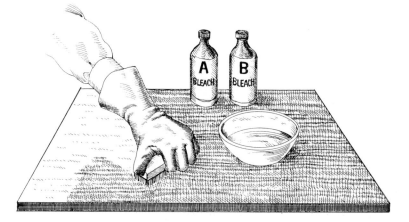

Two-solution chemical wood bleach is the most effective type for lightening dark woods. Wear rubber gloves to protect hands.

When working with any bleach, wear rubber gloves and old clothes with long sleeves to protect hands and arms. If bleach spills on exposed skin, wash immediately with lots of water.

After you've finished, throw out any bleach that remains in the bowl. Don't pour it back into the original bottle because it will ruin whatever's left for further use.

No matter what brand of bleach you use, or what it says on the label, it's always best to use a neutralizing rinse afterward. The simplest is ordinary white vinegar, and it works as well on two-solution bleaches as on laundry bleach.

First rinse the bleached piece with plain water. Then pour on vinegar, full strength, and let stand for a few minutes. Wipe off with clean rags and rinse with more water.

Instead of vinegar, you can use a borax solution as a neutralizer. (This works as well on oxalic acid as on any of the others.) Dissolve 1 cup borax in 1 quart of hot water, and apply to wood while still warm. Rinse off with clean water and allow wood to dry thoroughly before going ahead with any finish.

Since all bleaches have a water base, and since they have to be followed with a water rinse afterward, bleaching will almost always tend to raise the grain of the wood to some extent. This creates a slight fuzziness which can be removed after the wood is dry by rubbing lightly with fine sandpaper. If several bleaching applications will be required, don't do any sanding until after the final rinse.

After sanding, be sure you remove all dust by wiping down with a tack cloth (see page 45).

SPECIAL TOOLS FOR THE STRIPPER

SANDING MACHINES: Some purists still feel that the only way to do a proper job of smoothing fine wood is to do your sanding by hand. On some valuable antiques and heirlooms, this is probably the best way. However, for most projects with flat surfaces, sanding by machine is much faster and easier. True, you must be careful to avoid cutting too deeply or accidentally scratching the surface.

Electric sanding machines fall into three broad categories: disc sanders, belt sanders, and orbital sanders.

As its name implies, the *disc sander* consists of a round disc (usually made of hard rubber or flexible plastic) which has a replaceable abrasive disc fastened to its face. It is often sold as an accessory which you can use with an electric drill.

All disc sanders are suitable for rough work only (removing paint, smoothing surfaces around the outside of the house, etc.). They will scratch or gouge flat surfaces if not handled very carefully and so are virtually useless for most furniture finishing projects.

Belt sanders are powerful, fast-working machines that are heavier and more expensive than the other machines mentioned. They are preferred by some professionals for removing finishes on sizable areas, but they have to be used with great care on furniture. They work so fast it's easy to cut too deep in places. Never, but never, use a belt sander on veneer. It's too easy to cut completely through by simply holding the sander in one place for too long. Even on solid wood, keep the machine moving as long as the switch is depressed, and make sure you don't let it dip as you pass over an edge, or you'll wind up with rounded corners or edges.

Motor-driven *orbital sanders*, often referred to as finishing sanders, are probably the most useful all-round sanding machines for the furniture finisher. They have flat pads which accept sheets of abrasive paper (you cut conventional sheets into thirds or halves, depending on the model or brand).

Most orbital sanders move the pad in an oval pattern, but some permit straight-line action for final finishing. The sander cuts faster when moving in an oval pattern. The straight-line motion permits you to sand parallel to the grain, leaving the least possible number of scratches on the surface.

In addition to conventional motor-driven orbital sanders, there are also inex-

Belt sanders do a fast job of removing finishes and smoothing rough surfaces, but they can only be used on flat surfaces.

Orbital sanders, also known as finishing sanders, are generally easier to control than other power sanders, and are more useful in fine finishing.

pensive versions called "vibrator" models. They're powered by a type of vibrator, rather than a rotary electric motor. These lightweight, low-priced machines have a much shorter stroke than the orbital sanders, and they cut so slowly that there is hardly any advantage over conventional hand sanding. They are of little or no value in removing old finishes, or in smoothing down of even moderately rough surfaces. However, they are easier than hand sanding, so some may find them useful for fine smoothing.

Orbital and belt sanders are both available with dust catchers, either a small vacuum bag attached to collect most of the dust, or a connection that permits hooking up to a conventional shop or home vacuum cleaner while the machine is in use.

On belt sanders, these vacuum attachments are quite effective. They catch most of the dust created and minimize cleanup later on. On orbital sanders, however, the vacuum attachment is effective only on flat surfaces, and only when you don't override the edges, because an orbital sander equipped with a dust pickup attachment relies on a flexible suction "skirt" around its pad to pick up dust, and as soon as one corner or side of the machine rides over an edge the suction effect is lost.

When using any power-driven sanding machine, never make the common mistake of bearing down hard while the machine is working in an effort to make it cut faster. Pressing hard does just the opposite. It tends to overload the motor and actually makes the machine cut slower. It can also result in scorching the sandpaper and overheating the motor.

You can press down lightly to ensure firm contact with the work, but never so hard that you slow the machine down. On horizontal surfaces the weight of the machine is almost enough—just press lightly. On vertical surfaces you'll have to compensate for the weight of the machine and thus will have to apply a little more pressure.

For safety's sake it is a good idea to wear goggles with any electric sander—especially when working overhead. If the dust bothers you, wear a spray mask similar to the kind sold for use with paint sprayers. (Inexpensive, disposable models are sold in almost all paint and hardware stores.)

SCRAPERS: Hook-type scrapers, of the kind illustrated here, are useful for what finishers call rough work—taking off finishes. To use, hold the handle almost

Hook scraper.

parallel to the surface with one hand, while you bear down on the blade end with the other hand. Then drag the tool toward you. Use this tool cautiously until you get the feel of it, and don't try it with fine pieces. It's too easy to gouge the wood. Cabinetmaker's wood scrapers, available from mail-order houses, can also be useful, but some practice will be required before you learn how to use them. And don't forget the painter's scraper—it's good for taking off the glop left by chemical removers.

WIRE BRUSHES: Invaluable for degunking after using paint removers, especially carved and turned areas. Nothing scrubs up like these, and you'll want several in different sizes. Small rotary wire brushes that can be chucked into an electric drill can also come in handy for this kind of work.

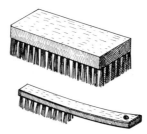

Wire brushes.

STEEL WOOL: This is a much finer abrasive than sandpaper, and you'll use a lot more elbow grease taking off a finish with it. It's likely to be more useful in the final smoothing operations, and for getting into curves, carvings, and turnings you can't work with sandpaper. We mention it here because it's also very useful for scraping off the leftovers of chemical removers, especially in those tricky areas. Like sandpaper, it's graded according to coarseness—3 is the coarsest, 1 is fine, and very fine grades go from 0 to 0000.

3 · Preparing for the New Finish—Or What to Fix First

IT's HARD TO DECIDE which should come first in a furniture-refinishing book—the chapter on stripping or the chapter on repairs—because some mending should be completed before stripping, some afterward, and sometimes it makes no difference at all.

The easy repairs—the kind most novices are likely to encounter—are almost always done afterward. I'm talking about surface repairs—the filling and patching of dents and gouges, smoothing of uneven areas, etc. For one thing, you will be better able to determine what needs to be done after the finish is off, and for another you wouldn't want some chemical or sandpaper prying your handiwork up along with the finish.

Loose joints—wobbly legs or spindles—are nothing for the beginner to be frightened of either. They are easily repaired the time-honored way—with glue, which is why they should be repaired *before* stripping if you're going to use a chemical remover. Because removers are liquid, they inevitably seep into the open cracks of loose joints, and not even a strong flushing with water or solvent will get all of the stuff out. The slightest residue will keep the glue from drying or bonding properly.

You could take the joint completely apart, without regluing, during the stripping process, and have greater success flushing out residue. Sometimes the joint doesn't come apart until the stripping process, and that's what you have to do. But it's best and safest to do it all first.

If you're stripping mechanically by sanding and scraping, then it makes no difference when you glue.

Of course, if you're not going to strip at all—if you're going to paint or antique—your repair problems are just a little different. Wood with a transparent or translucent finish shows blemishes, so you've got to be very careful about filling and patching in terms of color and how fillers match the wood, etc. But with an opaque finish, only smoothness counts, since nothing else shows. A bit of messy gluing can be covered over, but even here, neatness counts, because less sanding will be required. Following are other methods of repair that go along with gluing.

GLUING AND OTHER NAILLESS METHODS OF MENDING

Ever go antiquing with a real old-furniture nut? There's always lots of talk about dovetailing joints, pegging, and gluing—which all translates into: "Look, no nails or screws! It must be a good piece."

Those purists are almost always right. There are better and certainly more beautiful ways to put a piece of furniture together than with nails. Even if it should become necessary for the nonpurist—for practical reasons when there is no other choice—to use a screw or nail, it's rarely necessary for anyone to see it. Concealment, you'll discover, is very simple.

For starters, let's stick with the non-nail methods, which for your purposes mean gluing, and an occasional dowel.

When chair or table legs, or rungs, work loose from the holes in which they were fitted, the only way to do a thorough, permanent repair job on these joints is to take them apart completely so they can be properly reglued. I mean all the joints, not just the loose ones, because it's just too hard to take one joint apart without cracking or splitting the others.

When taking joints apart, by the way, watch for concealed screws, nails, and other fasteners. They're sometimes driven in from the side or back or at such an angle that they're almost impossible to detect if you don't look carefully, and they can really damage a good piece of wood if you don't find and remove them first.

Pry the joints apart by hand if you can, but you may use a rubber or plastic mallet, which won't mar the wood, to tap the pieces apart if necessary.

Most of the glues that were used years ago were not water-resistant and had an organic base, so if you find the joint difficult to take apart, you may be able to soften the old glue by wetting it with plenty of vinegar.

An even stronger solvent can be made by using glacial acetic acid (sold in photo supply stores), diluted with 3 or 4 parts of water. (When mixing acid with water, always pour the acid into the water rather than the water into the acid, and mix in a glass or plastic bowl. Concentrated acetic acid is very strong, so handle it with extreme care.)

After you have taken the joints completely apart, use a fine wood rasp or medium-grade sandpaper to clean the old glue off the ends of the rungs or legs, and use a pocketknife or similar tool to scrape all of the old glue out of the holes into which they fit. Sometimes hot water or vinegar will help clean out these recessed areas completely.

To reglue the joints you can use ordinary white glue that dries clear, such as

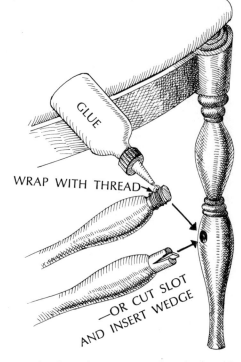

Two ways to insure a snug fit when rung fits loosely—wrap end with thread until it's the right thickness (above), or fit wedge into slot cut in end of rung beforehand (below). In both cases, coat with glue and then force into place.

Elmer's. But for a stronger bond and a "stickier" grip that will hold pieces in alignment more easily while you're setting them into position, use one of the pale-yellow or beige-colored aliphatic resin glues, which also come in plastic squeeze bottles and dry almost clear.

Either of these glues is adequate for most furniture repairs, but if you need exceptionally high strength or water resistance, then you will have to use a plastic resin glue, which comes in powder form. Its only drawback is that it is only effective in snug-fitting joints which have few, if any, voids. It also requires a longer clamping period than the white or yellow glues mentioned above, and clamping pressure must be uniformly applied along the entire joint in order to form a truly permanent bond.

Two-part epoxy glues are exceptionally strong, completely waterproof, and do not require clamping. All you have to do is keep the pieces in firm contact with each other while the adhesive sets. What's more, they have the ability to fill in voids when pieces fit loosely or when joints have decided gaps in them. However, they cost considerably more than other glues, and, worse, they form a dark-colored joint that is more noticeable when dry, so while they are okay for opaque finishes, they may not be suitable for transparent ones, on light woods.

When the end of a rung or leg has shrunk so much that it no longer fits snugly in its hole, there's no sense in merely pouring more wood glue into the joint. You have to take steps to make a snug fit first if you want to be sure the repair will be permanent and invisible. One easy method is to wrap the end of the loose-fitting member with fine cotton or linen thread to enlarge its diameter slightly. Then coat with glue and assemble in the usual manner.

Another way to do the job is to saw a slot in the end of the loose-fitting piece, then force a thin, wedge-shaped piece of wood into the slot as illustrated. When the piece is hammered into place, the wedge will be forced in and will spread the end of the loose-fitting rung slightly, expanding it enough to ensure a tight fit.

When reassembling pieces, coat each surface with glue and then clamp or tie the parts together to apply the pressure required to achieve a permanent bond.

Bar clamps or pipe clamps are useful for this kind of project. So are C-clamps and other woodworking clamps, which you'll learn more about later in this chapter. But if you don't have any of these handy, there are several other ways you can apply the needed pressure.

Where practical, simple weights (books, buckets of sand or water, bricks) set on top of a piece will do the trick.

In other cases, a rope tourniquet will serve almost as well as a professional web clamp. To make a rope tourniquet, wrap a piece of stout clothesline twice around the chair, drawer, or other piece being assembled. Then tie a knot to hold it in place. Pressure is applied by using a stick between the two turns of rope and then twisting, as pictured. Before doing this, insert pieces of heavy cardboard or similar padding over each corner to protect against damaging the wood as the rope tightens. Scrap pieces of cardboard or plywood should also be used under the jaws of all clamps to keep the metal from marring the wood.

There are many cases where it is impractical to take loose joints apart in order to do a proper job of regluing. Sometimes taking them apart will cause too much damage. Or perhaps only one or two joints are loose and it is not worth taking all the other joints apart.

In these cases, first force the pieces apart as much as you can without actually disjointing them. Then use a thin blade to scrape out as much of the old glue as possible. One tool that is handy for this job is a small fingernail file; another is a stiff piece of wire with a very small hook bent at the end.

Blow out as much of the dust and scrapings as possible. Then work glue into the joint with a piece of wire or a flexible artist's palette knife.

It helps if you can turn the piece so that the joint is vertical, with the open end up, so that gravity will help the glue flow down into it.

After you have worked in as much glue as possible, open and close the joint

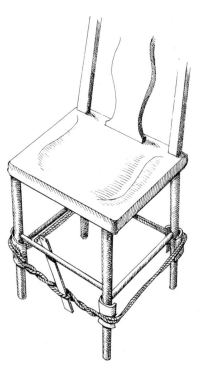

A rope tourniquet can be used instead of a web clamp to hold parts of a chair (or other piece of furniture) together while glue is setting.

a few times by pushing the loose pieces back and forth to spread the adhesive around on the inside. Then press the pieces together, and clamp them to apply the needed pressure while the glue sets.

A very handy gadget for working glue into a loose joint is a syringe type of glue injector—something that looks like the syringe that doctors use for hypodermic injections. Made of metal or plastic, and sold in many hardware stores as well as through mail-order houses that specialize in craftsmen's supplies, these tools have a narrow nozzle with a hole in the center. A plunger fits snugly inside the hollow barrel, which you fill with glue. Pushing on the plunger then forces the glue out through the nozzle.

To get the glue into the joint, drill a small hole where it will be the least noticeable—the back of a leg on a chair, under the seat for bench slats. Inject the glue through the hole so that it penetrates the joint. Keep pumping glue in until it oozes out around the assembled pieces. Apply clamping pressure and wipe off excess glue afterward. The little hole that remains will be filled with a wood or plastic compound later on.

There is one other method you can use to tighten a loose rung or similar joint when simple regluing doesn't seem to work. Drill a small hole completely through the joint, again in a not-too-visible place, and just big enough to drive a small dowel through it. It's easiest to match the hole to the dowel—if you have a ¼-inch dowel, use a ¼-inch drill. Next, work glue into the loosened joint

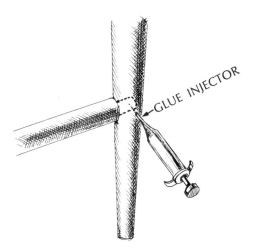

A syringe-type glue injector is used to force glue into a joint through a small hole drilled in an inconspicuous spot on part being repaired.

by one of the techniques just described. Then dip the dowel into more glue, and drive it home with a wood mallet.

The hole you drill for the dowel should be snug enough to ensure a tight fit, but not so tight that the dowel will be smashed when you try to drive it home. Your best bet is to drill trial holes in scrap material first to make sure you are using the right size bit for your particular dowel. To provide room for the glue, it helps to file a small flat area along the length of the dowel, using a rasp or piece of sandpaper. Cutting grooves lengthwise with a knife or fine saw is another method. Make the dowel longer than necessary and leave the excess sticking out until after the glue dries, then trim it off neatly with a hacksaw blade or coping saw and use sandpaper to contour the exposed part for a flush fit.

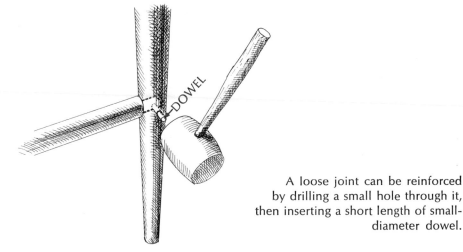

A loose joint can be reinforced by drilling a small hole through it, then inserting a short length of small-diameter dowel.

HIDING NAILS AND SCREWS WHEN YOU HAVE TO USE THEM

If you're working on a fine piece, repair it with dowels. But some pieces, for one reason or another, just don't merit the dowel treatment, so you will want to use small nails and screws. You're going to drill small pilot holes before driving the nails or screws in, so that you don't split the wood. The nails or screws will be driven in through the side of a joint, where they are least visible, so that's where you drill your holes. Again, try to work as much glue into the joint as you can before driving in the nails or screws.

Once a nail is in, you're going to countersink the head beneath the surface of the wood with a tool called a nailset and a hammer. The nailset is held on the nail and hit with the hammer to drive the nail head below the surface. To countersink screws, use a counterbore or drill bit that is the same diameter as the screw head. Drill a shallow hole just deep enough to permit recessing the screw's head below the wood's surface, but be careful to go no deeper than necessary. The holes left in each case will be filled later with matching wood plastic or colored patching compound to make them practically invisible.

There are even times when this kind of invisibility isn't quite necessary. Chairs and tables that have aprons or skirts beneath seat or top, for example, with legs that butt up against the underside, will often get wobbly because the brace that goes across the corner joint has worked loose. The brace may be a

Chair or table leg may be loose because wood brace (left) has worked loose and needs retightening–or because metal brace (right) needs to be tightened by taking up on wing nut in center.

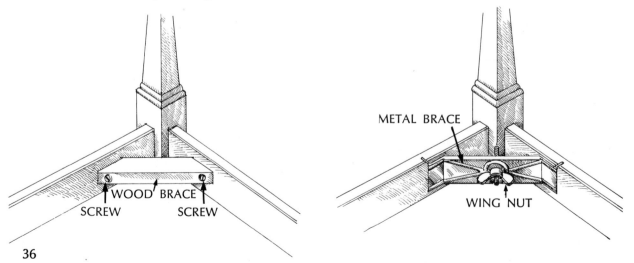

piece of wood secured by already visible screws driven into the frame on each side, or it may be a steel brace, with a threaded lag bolt going through the center to the inside corner of the leg.

In the latter case, tightening the wing nut will draw the assembly together more firmly. In the case of a wood brace, the screws may have worked loose and merely need tightening. If tightening the screws doesn't do the trick, or if the screws have gouged out oversized holes in the wood, then you may be better off installing a new wood block, slightly oversize, and securing this with both glue and screws.

VICTORY OVER VENEER PROBLEMS

Veneer, that thin layer of often gorgeous wood, bonded to a lesser wood, often develops special problems in time. The glue may come loose and the veneer will loosen and lift in spots. Or sometimes a small rip along one of the edges can turn into a large peeling problem.

Blistering and lifting repairs are not very difficult. Replacing a missing piece can be a bit trickier, but not impossible.

If the veneer is loose along one edge, pry it up carefully and slide a knifeblade or fingernail file under it to scrape out as much of the old glue as you can. An emery board, the kind used on fingernails, is especially handy for jobs of this kind. Just be very careful not to lift the veneer any more than necessary to avoid splitting or cracking it.

Use a soda straw to blow all dust and dried glue flakes out from under the veneer, then work fresh glue underneath by poking it in with a piece of wire or a knifeblade. Ordinary white glue is probably the easiest material to use, since it dries clear and is virtually nonstaining.

After the glue has been spread around as much as possible, move the loose veneer up and down a few times to make certain both surfaces are coated. Now press down hard and use clamps or weights to keep the two surfaces in contact until the glue dries. Be sure you wipe off excess glue that oozes out before it dries. It will be difficult to remove later on.

If the veneer is loose in the center of a panel, creating a noticeable blister, use a *very sharp* knife to slit through the middle of the blister. Then press one half down while you work glue under the other half with a thin spatula or piece of wire. (An artist's palette knife, with a thin, long, flexible blade, is ideal for this job.)

After you have spread glue under one half of the blister, press that half down and then work glue in under the other side.

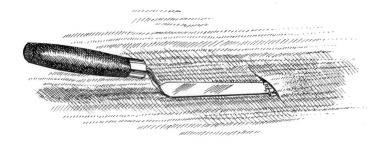

A blister in veneer can often be cured by cutting a slit across the middle, then working glue under each half and pressing flat with weights or clamps.

———————————

Now press the entire blister up and down several times to spread the glue around and apply weights or clamps to hold both sides of the veneer in place while the glue hardens. To keep the weights or clamps from sticking to the surface (some glue will ooze up through the slit you made in the middle of the blister), cover the veneer with a piece of waxed paper, after wiping off as much as possible of the oozed-up glue with a damp cloth. There will be a barely visible slit, but on old pieces it sort of adds to the antique look.

When a piece of veneer is missing entirely, the only way to make a repair that won't be noticeable is to insert a patch of the same veneer. There are very few lumberyards that stock wood veneer these days, but it can be ordered from some mail-order houses that cater to home craftsmen, as well as from some dealers that specialize in cabinetmaker's supplies.

However, since wood is a natural product, even if you can find the veneer, chances are it won't match the tone and grain of your surface exactly, so in many cases you are better off trying to remove a small piece of veneer—enough to make the patch you need—from the same piece of furniture. You do this by cutting out a piece in a place where it is not easily visible. For example, the back of a piece may be covered with the same veneer, or there may be veneer on the inside of a door or drawer front. Sometimes you can even get away with cutting a piece out of one side of a large unit that stands in a corner or against another large piece. A small patch of veneer removed from the hidden side, near the back or near the floor, won't be noticeable.

The easiest way to "steal" such a piece is to cut it out near an edge. This will enable you to slide a knife or sharp chisel in from that edge in order to lift off a small piece of the veneer.

If this is not practical, then you can use a sharp knife to cut out a rectangular or oblong piece that will be large enough to make the size patch needed. Use a metal straightedge to guide your knife and cut along each side three or four

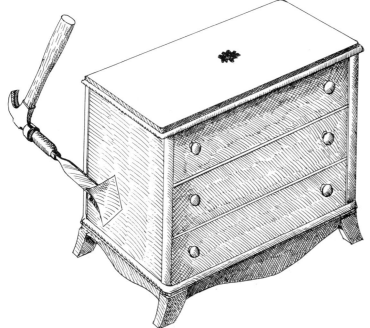

When a piece of matching veneer cannot be found, it may pay to cut out a piece where it will not show, and use it for making a repair in a prominent area.

times to make certain the piece will lift out cleanly. Then carefully slide chisel or knife blade under this cutout section to slice the glue away until you can lift it out neatly.

The next step is to trim this piece to a neat rectangle, square, or diamond shape, so that when laid over the area where the veneer is missing, the new piece will fully cover it.

If you have a choice, try for a diamond-shaped patch with the grain running in the long direction of the diamond. This shape tends to blend in more easily than a rectangular or square that has one edge running straight across the direction of the grain.

After the patch has been trimmed to a size slightly larger than the damaged area, lay it directly over the damage and trace its outline onto the existing veneer with the point of an awl or icepick. Now lay the patch aside and carefully cut out the old veneer to match the pattern just outlined.

Don't cut on the outside of the line. If anything, cut slightly inside the line. You can always trim the patch slightly if needed to make a snug fit. Be particularly careful about matching the direction of the general grain pattern. If trimming is needed, use a single-edge razor blade until the patch drops neatly into the area where the damaged veneer has been cut out.

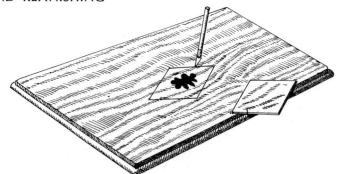

Trace outline of patch over damaged area. Then cut out piece to be replaced with a sharp knife.

Use hammer with knife or very sharp chisel to gently pry off piece that is damaged in the center.

After the old veneer has been removed, scrape the dried glue out from underneath, blow all dust away, and glue the new patch in its place. Use weights or clamps to apply pressure until the glue sets, and wipe away any glue that may have oozed out. The hairline seam or joint will fill in when the new finish is applied and—if you have worked carefully—should be scarcely noticeable when the job is done.

Scrape out all old glue, apply fresh glue, and fit new patch into place. Old piece can be reinserted in place where new patch was cut out (side or back), and damage may be scarcely noticeable there.

PATCHING CRACKS, HOLES, DENTS, AND GOUGES

Some old pieces of furniture have "distress" marks that add to the character and appearance of the piece and should be left as is when refinishing. However, there are times when scratches, dents, gouges, and other defects are just plain unsightly and should be patched or smoothed over if you want the final finish to have a smooth, professional look.

Patching compounds for filling cracks, holes, and gouges in wood are sold in most paint and hardware stores, lumberyards, and home centers. They generally fall into one of two categories: ready-mixed plastic compounds that dry quickly, and powdered compounds which you mix with water to form a putty-like material for use on wood.

Generally, the powdered wood-putty compounds are available only in a kind of light tan or buff color that is fine for opaque finishes, while ready-mixed wood plastics (also referred to as wood dough) come in a variety of wood-tone shades so you can blend them in better with different-colored woods and finishes.

These wood patching compounds differ in porosity when hard—that is in their ability to absorb stain. Some are fairly porous and will "take" stains to some degree, while others are extremely hard and dense and will not absorb any stain at all. This means you have to be very careful about using them on a piece that you plan to eventually treat with stain. The stain will not be absorbed uniformly, so that all the patch marks can stand out when the job is done, or the stain may not "take" at all on any of the patched areas.

For best results, it's smart to experiment beforehand with various brands and types. Make some gouges on a few pieces of scrap wood, then apply the patching material and let it dry hard. Sand smooth and apply stain over this to see how the patch absorbs the stain. Don't rely on a manufacturer's claims that its filler absorbs stain. Even if it does, it won't absorb it in exactly the same way as the wood around it.

The usual way to avoid this headache is to apply the stain to the wood first, then use a colored filler or patching compound that matches the stained wood when dry. If you can't find a patching compound to match the color of your stained wood, remember that colors can be intermixed or "doctored" by adding tinting colors, which you can buy in most paint stores. This will take some experimenting, especially since patching compounds dry to a different shade than they appear in the can. But this is really the only way you can be sure what the final results will look like, and you'll learn a lot in the process.

Never try to fill a deep crack or gouge with a single application of patching compound. Although some of these materials are labeled "nonshrinking," most will contract to some degree when applied in heavy layers. Also, they may not dry properly if you put them on in thick layers. The compound dries at the surface first and remains soft underneath for quite a while. To prevent this, apply the material in layers, allowing each one to harden before applying the next one. The last layer should be slightly higher than the surrounding surface so that you can trim it flush by sanding or shaving carefully with a very sharp chisel or scraper.

To increase strength of bond when patching broken corners or edges, drive very small staples or brads partway into the wood first, making sure heads won't stick up above the surface. These will help ensure a firm grip on the compound when it hardens.

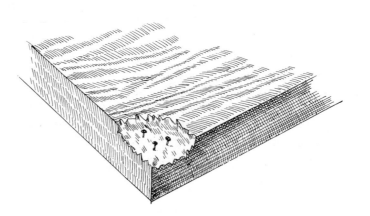

When using any of these compounds to build up a chipped edge or corner, you can increase the strength of the patch by drilling a few small holes in the bottom of the recess or cavity before applying the first layer of patching material. As you press the compound into position, with a little extra pressure you'll force some of it into the holes, increasing the strength of the bond.

A better method is to drive a few small staples or brads into the cavity, allowing the heads to protrude slightly—but not high enough to interfere with the smoothing over of the final patch. When the wood plastic is packed around the staples or brads, the heads will firmly lock the patch into place and greatly reduce the chances of its being knocked or chipped away later on.

SANDING FOR SMOOTHNESS

Unless you're really lucky, and the stripping process has left you with a satin finish, the last step before applying any finish is the final sanding and smoothing. This requires more care when refinishing an old piece than it does when applying any finish to a new piece. On new wood your only concern is to get the wood as smooth as possible—no matter how much sanding is required. On old pieces, you want to retain that aged patina we've talked so much about.

Patina or not, if the surfaces involved are sizable and relatively flat (a tabletop, for example) then the work will go a lot faster if you use an electric sander. (See Chapter 2, "Sanding Machines," page 26.) Use an orbital finishing sander for the final smoothing, but handle it with care to avoid cutting any deeper than absolutely necessary, especially on edges and corners. The paper you use should be 150. Hand sanding over this with 220 paper will give you a satin-smooth finish.

On most small surfaces, and on older pieces where you have to be especially careful, hand sanding is probably the safest and simplest procedure. Even if you use a finishing sander for preliminary smoothing, it's still advisable to switch to hand sanding for the final smoothing.

On curved, carved, or contoured surfaces, steel wool works better than sandpaper. It's less likely to leave scratch marks in the wood than sandpaper. It is slower-working and takes more rubbing to do the same job, but it does give much better control.

For round pieces, such as legs or spindles, you can tear the steel wool in long strips, and then use it shoeshine-style. Grab each end with one hand and pull back and forth, maintaining a steady pressure on each end.

You can do the same with fairly fine sandpaper. Simply cut the paper into long strips, and follow the directions above. To keep the strips from tearing, reinforce the backs with strips of cellophane tape.

If you're going to sand by hand instead of machine, start on the raw wood with 100 or 120 paper. Sand at a slight angle to the direction of the grain, but no more than necessary to level off any ridges or scratches left after stripping. Then switch to 220, this time working parallel to the grain wherever possible so no visible scratches remain.

As mentioned earlier, 220 paper can give you a satin-smooth finish, but you can go on to an even silkier surface with 280 or 320 paper. Before switching to this fine grade, wipe the surface clean with a rag lightly moistened with paint thinner to get rid of any grit left by the coarser papers. Now once again go with the grain.

Whatever grade of paper you use for the final smoothing, check the surface frequently with your fingertips. You can feel rough spots more easily than you can see them. You can also hold a bright light behind the surface, and almost parallel to it. This angular light will show up the slightest irregularities.

And remember, when hand sanding on a flat surface, it's best to use a sanding block (see page 15).

On some types of wood, especially in the softer varieties, sanding with even the finest grit does not always leave the surface perfectly smooth, because the wood fibers tend to stand up along the grain. This creates a fuzzy surface that never really looks or feels smooth. Sometimes this isn't noticeable until the first coat of stain has been applied, while in other cases it can be clearly seen even on the raw wood. Here's an old preventive trick that many professional finishers use. Just before the final sanding dampen the wood slightly by wiping with a sponge that has been moistened in water. The water will cause the wood fibers on the surface to swell slightly, so that when they dry, these fibers will remain erect. The final sanding will remove this fuzz and leave the surface very smooth. It also minimizes the likelihood of more grain-raising when the stain is applied.

If the wood is very soft and fuzzy, here's another method that may work even better. Dilute some 4-pound-cut shellac with 2 parts of denatured alcohol. (The "pound-cut" of shellac is explained on page 73.) Apply a very thin "wash" coat to the surface. Avoid overlapping strokes with a brush. You want to make sure the wood gets only one coat over its entire surface.

The shellac will not only raise fibers, which can be sanded down, it will also partially seal the surface and tend to stabilize the grain and make it uniform in porosity. The fibers will be locked firmly in position so they can no longer swell when stain or other liquid coatings are applied. Partially sealing the grain also helps ensure that a wood stain applied over it will "take" uniformly. No more blotchy spots where the stain soaks in more rapidly in some places than it does in others, a common problem with very soft wood.

If there are deeply embedded discolorations that will not come out with ordinary surface sanding—without damaging the wood or changing its contours —use a bleach (see page 23) before the final sanding.

After sanding, it is important that you remove every bit of dust and grit before you apply the first coat of stain, sealer, or other finishing material. Slight specks and fine dust particles, which may be practically invisible on the raw wood, will stand out conspicuously after a finish has been applied. They will ruin the appearance of any finish, no matter how hard you work.

Wiping the surface down with a dry cloth or brushing the dust off is not enough. Using a vacuum cleaner is better, but even this will not remove all of the dust.

The best thing to do is vacuum to remove the heaviest accumulations. Then wipe the entire surface down carefully with a "tack rag."

Sold in most paint stores as well as in many hardware stores, and often referred to as a "tacky cloth," a tack rag is nothing more than a piece of coarse-mesh cotton or cheesecloth which has been impregnated with a varnish-and-oil mixture to make it sticky. It picks up dust without leaving any residue on the surface of the wood.

To use the tack rag, fold it to a convenient size and wipe it over the surface

To make a tack rag, wet folded cheesecloth with water, sprinkle with turpentine, add a few drops of varnish, and knead well.

of the wood carefully. Don't skip any spots. As the exposed side of the cloth gets loaded with dust, keep folding it to expose a fresh surface.

If you cannot find tack rags in your local paint or hardware store, make your own out of a piece of cheesecloth. Start by folding the fabric into a pad and wetting it with water. Then squeeze almost dry.

Next, with the damp cloth still folded, pour a little turpentine over the fabric and work this into the cloth by squeezing or kneading it with your hands.

Now with the cloth still folded flat, pour a small amount of varnish over the fabric, or sprinkle it through the folds. (Use about 1 ounce of varnish for a piece of fabric that's about a yard square when completely unfolded.)

Work this varnish through the pad, again by kneading the cloth with your hands, until the varnish has spread uniformly through the entire piece of cloth.

Unfold it to see if there are any dry spots remaining, and if so, sprinkle on a little more varnish and knead again. The cloth should be uniformly amber or light-yellow in color and damp enough to feel kind of sticky. But it should not be so damp that it drips liquid when squeezed hard.

The tack rag is now ready for use. Store the rag in a tightly closed screw-top jar or airtight plastic bag which will keep it from drying out.

SPECIAL TOOLS FOR THE FIXER

WOOD CLAMPS: A few *C-clamps* and a couple of *bar clamps* will be needed when regluing pieces or repairing breaks and splits. You can sometimes get by with simply placing weights on glued pieces, or by wrapping with heavy string or

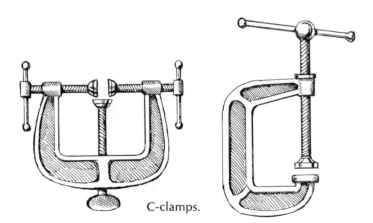

C-clamps.

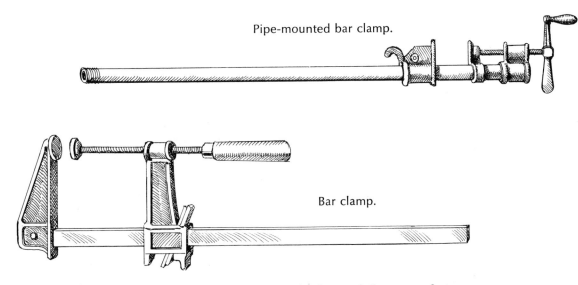

Pipe-mounted bar clamp.

Bar clamp.

light rope. But on most jobs, the only way to apply the needed pressure between two glued pieces will be to use a clamp of some kind. Particularly useful is a *web clamp* that can be wrapped completely around a loose chair or cabinet. It has a ratchet mechanism that you can tighten with a wrench to apply as much pressure as desired around bulky or odd-shaped objects.

Web clamp.

SCREWDRIVERS: You should have a fairly complete assortment of these in various sizes, two with Phillips-type blades (large and small), and the rest with flat blades. In addition to different blade widths you will also want several very

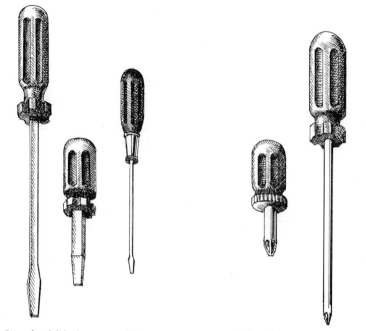

Standard-blade screwdrivers.   Phillips-blade screwdrivers.

short models or "stubby" types for reaching into places where an ordinary screwdriver will not fit.

CHISELS: Two or three wood chisels in different sizes will come in handy for trimming pieces to fit when patches or repairs must be made, as well as for making joints when parts must be replaced or rebuilt prior to reassembling them. If you buy a set of chisels in three sizes—½-inch, ¾-inch, and 1-inch in blade width—you will have everything you need, but make sure they are always kept well sharpened.

Wood chisels.

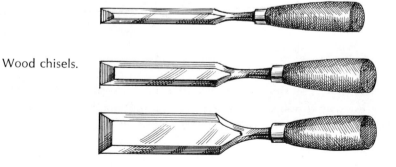

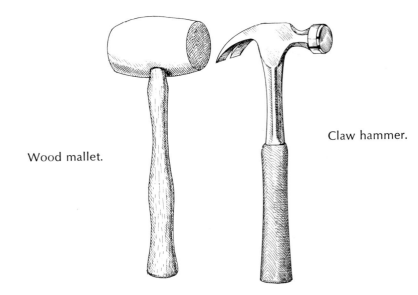

Wood mallet.

Claw hammer.

HAMMER: Actually you will want two hammers—a conventional carpenter's claw hammer and a wood mallet with a plastic or rubber face that you can use for light pounding when forcing pieces together or assembling joints.

HANDSAWS: A small, fine-tooth dovetail saw will be needed for cutting pieces to precise size, and for trimming moldings when making joints. A coping saw will also come in handy for making curved cuts and for trimming pieces of veneer to size when necessary. For really extensive repairs, or for rebuilding damaged pieces, a regular carpenter's saw, or an electric saber saw, will also be needed.

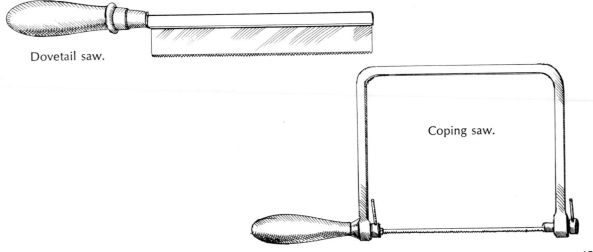

Dovetail saw.

Coping saw.

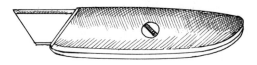

Utility knife.

UTILITY KNIFE: One of the most frequently used tools is a very sharp knife. A good pocket knife will do, but your best bet is a so-called utility knife of the type that uses disposable blades which are razor-sharp, yet inexpensive, and can be quickly replaced when they become dull.

WOOD RASPS: Ofter needed as a preliminary to the use of sandpaper or other abrasive materials, one or two rasps in different sizes and shapes should be included. They will reach into places where sandpaper or a scraper can't, and they help speed the job of trimming pieces to fit when joining parts that have been replaced. In addition to the conventional rasps, one or two half-round and round models in different sizes are necessary. Select these with medium to fine teeth, rather than the very coarse ones used by carpenters.

Wood rasps.

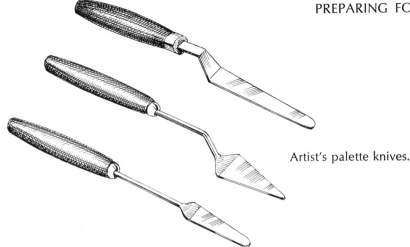

Artist's palette knives.

FOR APPLYING AND SMOOTHING THE PATCHING COMPOUNDS: You'll need a good-quality, flexible putty knife, about 1½ or 2 inches wide, made of springy, polished steel, with a straight, sharp edge. This tool is not for scraping, just for patching and smoothing. For scraping and other rough work you can use a less expensive, stiff-bladed knife which does not have such a sharp edge, and which can be 2 to 3 inches in width.

An artist's palette knife is another handy tool for smoothing, filling, and applying patching compounds in small cracks and in tight corners. Sold in all stores that sell art supplies, these palette knives come in different sizes and shapes. Trowel-shaped models are generally the most useful.

MISCELLANEOUS: These are the pushers, pullers, tracers, and make-fitters that come in handy at the oddest—and most crucial—repair moments. They probably should be in everybody's tool chest. Most useful are pliers—both needlenose and slip-joint. For tracing and punching tiny holes, the awl takes first place. When you need just a fraction of an inch off, and the sanding isn't doing it fast enough, a plane comes in very handy.

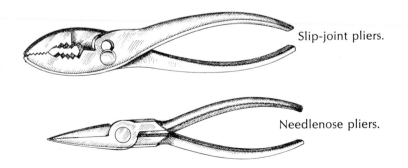

Slip-joint pliers.

Needlenose pliers.

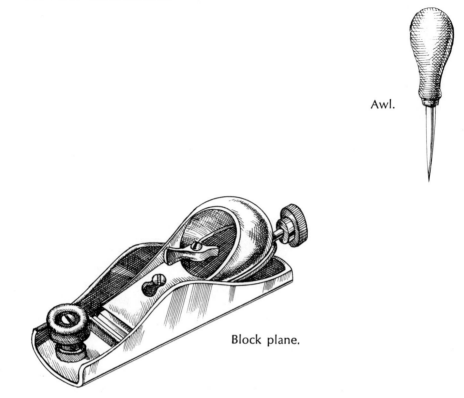

Awl.

Block plane.

ELECTRIC SANDERS: See page 27.

4 · When Bare Wood Is *Almost* Enough

SOME WOODS ARE SO BEAUTIFULLY AGED or have such a naturally attractive tone and shade that no staining or bleaching is required. More often than not, however, a stain of some kind will be needed to strengthen or deepen color, accent grain, make mismatching parts of a piece blend together, or add character.

There are lots of good reasons to stain, and basically only one good reason not to, and if you've got an experienced eye or your piece has luckily come "clean" of its old finish without too much stripping, you can tell the difference at a glance. The trouble is that sometimes, especially to the uninitiated who haven't seen too much wood without a finish, the stripped-down piece can look disappointing. It's a bit too dull with no fire or glow, has a dryish quality, and it's not always easy to tell by eye whether just a clear finish will do the trick, or a little judicious staining is needed to bring it all to life. But even the experienced don't always make that decision by sight alone. There's an easier way.

WHEN BARE WOOD IS ENOUGH

It's the oldest trick in the world, sometimes known among finishers as the "spit" test. Wipe a damp rag across a smooth, flat portion of your piece, and under good light, take a careful look at the wet wood. That's very close to what it will look like with just a clear finish on it, only better. So if you love what you see, turn to Chapter 5, which follows, and find out what the clear finishes are, and what they can do for you.

Even if you *almost* love the look of your wood when it's wet, it might pay at this point to look at the finishes before you make any staining decisions. Most finishes tend to darken wood a little. Some have an amber cast and some a bit of orange, so if it's just a little color deepening you're after, or a touch of mellow gold or yellow, or a bit more fire in the glow, could be you can still skip the staining step.

WHEN AND WHY TO STAIN

For most home finishers, staining problems fall into two major categories—getting the wood to look the way it's "supposed" to, or changing it considerably to suit either your taste or some specific purpose.

It's amazing how few people associate raw wood from the lumberyard with the same wood used in making furniture. Take that "beautifully aged" look described at the beginning of this chapter: to many, that's the way wood is "supposed" to look, so it comes as a surprise that only time and careful handling, or some other process, has given the piece its richness and character.

The other process, of course, is staining, and while it won't enable you to reproduce a century-old patina exactly, it can give you a richness of color and grain that's a terrific imitation.

Even if new wood is your idea of beauty—as natural as you can get it—a light stain, just enough to strengthen color and highlight grain, can give a less-than-prime piece of lumber a lot of character.

Wood stains have also been used for years to "upgrade" wood—to make a relatively inexpensive or unfashionable species look like something "better." It was back in colonial America that pine began masquerading as mahogany, so beloved back in Europe, or walnut, which ran a close second.

These days, the attempt is likely to be a way to get the odd or inexpensive piece to match the wood in the rest of the room, rather than self-conscious upgrading of single pieces or roomsful of furniture. All the same, you're likely to get as good results as they did long ago, especially on the less-dense hardwoods, such as elm, poplar, and gum, which take stain well and have very little grain pattern of their own to clash with the grains of other woods.

Which brings us to a warning for every novice finisher. Stain changes only the *color* of the wood, not its grain pattern. True, color may be the first thing most people will notice, but some species have such a distinctive grain pattern that any attempt to duplicate their appearance by mere stain is almost certain to result in disappointment.

That doesn't necessarily mean a camouflaged piece will look bad. As some of those old mahogany-finished pine pieces will attest, wood, like fabric, is not a slave to color. You may even get some diverse pieces to go very well together in terms of color alone, especially when they're low on grain. But if you try to use a walnut or mahogany stain to make an inexpensive pine piece look as if it actually were made of walnut or mahogany, don't expect to fool anyone who knows much about wood.

There's another good reason why stain is sometimes used on furniture made of several different types of wood, or pieces that are not uniform in tone or color. A dark stain will often help blend these lighter and darker parts together for a more consistent overall tone before finishing.

In all "matching-type" problems, of course, you must remember that a stain will look different on different types of wood. Walnut on pine, for example, does not always look the same as walnut on walnut—or even the same from one piece of walnut to the next. The examples given here do take stains most easily and truly, and we'll discuss more specific problems and how to solve them when we get down to the stains themselves.

PRESEALING SOFT WOODS AND SOFTER EDGES FOR BETTER COVERAGE

Many hardwoods have a uniform density of grain, which allows stain to soak in evenly over the entire surface—except where end grain is exposed. End grain occurs where the wood was cut across or against the grain—the ends of shelves, for example, or table rims and edges. End grain is very porous, so stain will soak into it very quickly, penetrate very deeply, and make it look much darker than the rest of the wood.

The same thing happens when staining some types of softwoods, like pine and fir, which have alternating layers of hard and soft grain, and alternating areas of porosity. You wind up with a streaky, blotchy, "wild" grain effect which is a lot less interesting than it sounds, and definitely unattractive.

There is a cure. A thin coat of sealer is applied first—thin enough to seal the surface only partially so that the stain doesn't soak in too deeply in porous areas. It's important *not* to seal the wood completely. You want to limit the stain's penetration, not prevent it.

If you're not sure whether a sealer is needed, test the stain first on a scrap piece of the same kind of wood, or on the back or bottom of the piece. If doubt persists, seal. It's safer, and you can always compensate for slower penetration by using a darker stain, or applying additional coats of your chosen color.

The two products most often used to seal porous wood are thinned shellac and penetrating wood sealer.

Professionals generally prefer a "wash" coat of shellac. It dries very quickly, for one thing, and you can stain over it in about an hour. It's made by mixing 4 parts denatured alcohol with 1 part 4-pound-cut shellac. (You'll learn more about various "pound-cuts" of shellac in the next chapter, on clear finishes. The 4-pound-cut is very widely available.)

Brush the shellac wash on rapidly with a wide brush, making every effort not to overlap or cover any area more than once. A clean, thin, one-layer sweep is what you want. Because shellac dries so quickly, overlapping, or even too much brushing back and forth, can result in some spots getting two coats of shellac instead of one, which means some spots are sealed more than others, and gone is that uniform staining job you've just taken this extra step to ensure. As a rule, a light rubdown with very fine steel wool, before the first coat of stain is applied, will help.

If all those precautions about overlapping have you feeling a bit nervous, here's another method that's much safer for the amateur. You'll have to wait a bit longer for it to dry, but it could be worth it. It's easier to control, and there's less likelihood of buildup.

Mix 1 part penetrating wood sealer (a finish you'll be hearing a lot more about) with 2 parts paint thinner, and brush on over the surface. Wait a minute or so, and wipe down with a clean cloth to remove any excess still on the surface. Allow it to try overnight before applying wood stain.

THE STAINS—FROM FAILPROOF AND FABULOUS TO TOP PRO METHODS BUT TRICKY

Wood stains are a lot like fabric dyes. They soak in and tint the wood fibers, without hiding the texture. Unlike opaque finishes such as paint, they allow natural grains and even some color to show through—the exact degree varying with the type of stain used. Stains run the gamut from translucent to totally transparent, from easy-to-use to tricky, and each has its special uses.

Everybody who's been refinishing furniture for any length of time has heard about staining formulas containing everything from shoe polish to chewing tobacco to snake oil, and there's always some perfectly reliable human being swearing that it really works. But whatever mysterious brews ultimately get thrown together, the stains you're most likely to use fall into three broad categories: pigmented stains, sometimes called pigmented wiping stains; penetrating or dye-type stains; and powdered aniline stains designed to be mixed with water or alcohol.

Pigmented stains are made up of tiny particles of pigment suspended in either an oil or an emulsion-type latex base. The pigments never really dissolve, which means the stain has to be stirred frequently when you're using it, or the particles will settle to the bottom of the container, and your stain will vary in both consistency and color.

But that's about the hardest thing you'll have to do with this stain. It's the easiest to use, forgiving of errors to the point where it's practically foolproof. If you think you've put too much on, you can usually wipe off as much as you want, if you rub promptly with a dry cloth, or a rag saturated with paint thinner. Since pigmented stains don't penetrate as deeply or as quickly as the dye types, there's very little likelihood of streaking or lap marks, and if you don't love what you see, sanding can take some of the color off even after the piece has dried.

There are drawbacks to stains that don't penetrate very deeply. They will fade more quickly if exposed to sunlight, for example, and they're not as transparent or clear as the penetrating dye-type stains, so color tends to be a bit "cloudier" when dry. The tiny particles of solid pigment will also partially conceal or "cloud" some of the grain, which can be an advantage on poor-quality woods. But the fact of the matter is that it never really looks bad on any wood.

There's very little difference between oil-base pigmented stain (loosely referred to as an oil stain) and latex-base pigmented stain, except that the latter can be thinned with water, and that means you can also clean your tools and hands with water, which is a definite plus. But don't let this mislead you into thinking that this is a "water" stain, which is a totally different beast, as you'll soon discover.

Penetrating oil stains are basically wood dyes. No pigments or any other solid particles in suspension here. Colors are completely dissolved, which makes this type of stain much more transparent and brilliant in color than pigmented stains. No grain is hidden, and the dye penetrates pretty deeply into the wood, making it far more resistant to fading.

Most of the penetrating stains available ready-mixed from the local paint store have an oil base, and are marked with the words "penetrating" or "dye-type" on the label so you can't mistake them for pigmented stains.

On really fine furniture made of good-quality wood, penetrating-type stains are always preferable to pigmented stains. They not only allow everything to show through, they're not as likely to mask a patina if used judiciously.

So what's the catch? They're not quite as foolproof as the pigmented stains. On the less expensive or softer woods, or pieces that have an uneven porosity due to surface damage of some sort, a preliminary coat may be needed to avoid blotchiness. This type of stain will penetrate far more deeply in the softer parts of the grain than it will in the denser parts. (In case you've forgotten about presealing, see page 55.)

Powdered water stains are aniline-type wood dyes. You buy them in powder form, and dissolve them in water or alcohol. Widely preferred by professionals because they dry very quickly and provide the clearest, purest color and deepest fiber penetration, they can be very tricky for the amateur. They're not widely available except by mail order, and you have to do a bit of by-guess-and-by-golly when you mix anything yourself. But there are more important objections:

(1) They raise the grain of the wood, so you not only have to sponge with water and sand the wood before the stain has been applied, you also have to rub down with fine sandpaper after the stain has been applied.

(2) They dry very quickly, so you have to be careful about lapping or streaking when putting them on with a brush (professionals prefer to spray them on); amateurs find it difficult to achieve uniform results.

(3) Most important, perhaps, water stains are not suitable for use on old wood that has been previously finished. Even if all of the old finish has been carefully stripped off, water stains often will not penetrate properly and you'll wind up with a blotchy, uneven effect that's difficult to correct.

Powdered aniline-type stains that are designed for mixing with alcohol rather than water dry even faster. They have the advantage of not raising the grain the way a water stain will, but they are even harder to apply evenly, because they dry so quickly that it is almost impossible to brush them out smoothly— even on moderate-size surfaces. It is my firm conviction that amateur refinishers are better off staying away from them.

All the same, they can be important and are beautiful, so you may want to experiment. And there are certain finishes you may want to use that just won't work with any other stain—a French polish, for example (see page 73).

CHOOSING A COLOR

You can't simply wipe a stain entirely off the surface of wood and start from scratch if you don't like the color. You can come pretty close with pigmented stains, but some of it always soaks into the fibers, and it would take some sanding, rather than just a wipe, to get it all out. Which means that unless you want to do a sanding job, or get out the bleach, or go a lot darker than you really want to, it's important to go through the trouble of picking the right color to start with.

How to choose? Manufacturers supply color cards and stores display samples, but you can't let them be your only guide. Unlike paint, which is opaque and looks the same on all surfaces, stain is very much affected by the color of the wood that shows through. Stains also "take" differently on different pieces of wood—sometimes of the same kind.

Some manufacturers try to show you what several different stains look like on a variety of woods, but the variety is rarely broad enough, and the samples often don't look like real wood. The best way to be sure is to actually try the stain on the same type of wood as your piece, or a very similar one. Unless you're working with a very unusual kind of wood, chances are you can get some scraps from the local lumberyard. In fact, if you find yourself fascinated by refinishing (it happens a lot), and plan on doing more of it, it might behoove you to begin a collection of the most popular cabinet woods and softwoods used in furniture. Some of them might be raw and new, not stripped or aged like some of the pieces you'll be working with, but they'll give a better idea of what's going to happen than a sample card will.

Barring scrap pieces, try your stain on an inconspicuous part of your piece—back, bottom, or corner—where discoloration left over by the wrong stain won't be noticed.

Unfortunately, there is no standardization of names to describe colors between different companies. One brand's black walnut may be very different from another's. In fact, the same colors by one manufacturer may vary from batch to batch.

The lesson to be learned here is that if you find a color you like, and you're planning to use it on a big piece or a whole suite of furniture, buy enough for the whole job. Then, before you begin, mix all the cans together. It's your only way to ensure perfect matching.

If you don't find a ready-mixed shade you like, don't be afraid to mix two or three colors together. In many cases, it's the only way to find a shade you like. Once you find it, don't forget to mix up a batch of it big enough to finish your project.

Don't forget, no wood, not even a freshly stained piece, looks the way it will with a finish on it. You could give your piece the "spit" test, described on page 53. But if you've got scraps with stain tests on them, why not try the actual finishes over them? You'd be surprised what a finish with an amber or orange cast can do. Even a supposedly perfectly clear finish makes a big difference.

STAINING TECHNIQUES

Except for some special preparation for water stains, methods of applying most stains are pretty much the same. They can be put on with a brush, rag, sponge, or one of the flat painting pads that are so popular today. Whatever's most comfortable and gives you the best and most uniform coverage is right.

Generally, after a few minutes excess stain is wiped off with a rag. Most stains should be wiped for uniformity of color, but exactly how long you wait before ragging it off depends on the type of stain you're using, the porosity of the wood, and the depth of color you're after. A penetrating stain, for example, soaks into wood more rapidly than a pigmented product, and should generally be wiped sooner.

There is no set rule that governs how long you should wait before wiping. Just don't wait so long that you can't wipe. Otherwise, only experimentation and experience with similar stains and woods will tell you how long to wait. Just remember that it's easier to correct the effects of wiping off too soon—with another coat or a darker stain—than it is to sand, bleach, and otherwise strenuously lighten a piece on which the stain's been left too long.

Start by applying the stain to a small section of wood at a time. Begin wiping with a dry rag as soon as the wood looks dark enough. If you find yourself removing too much of the stain, try waiting a little longer. If this doesn't help, you may have to switch to a darker stain. Or you can darken your original stain by adding tinting pigments available in most paint stores. (More about pigments coming up in the discussion of wood fillers on page 62.)

When you're dealing with matching problems, like lighter and darker woods next to each other on the same piece, you can control the final effect to some extent by wiping the dark piece sooner or more vigorously than the other. Or you can first stain the lighter piece with a stain that will bring it closer to the darker wood in tone. After the stain dries, apply another coat over both pieces, which should eliminate any differences in color that remain.

To prepare wood for aniline or water-stain dyes, follow the suggestions on page 44 for getting a soft wood smooth, with no fuzzy wood fibers sticking up. Only this time, dampen the wood—all of it—with a sponge moistened in warm water. After the piece has dried, sand as you would for a final sanding. This will probably eliminate any grain-raising after staining. If not, you'll sand again. Since staining does not tend to be uniform with this type of dye, sanding may help you control color. You can always stain again for a darker color, but keeping an entirely even tone won't be easy. As mentioned, pros spray this stain on for uniform effect. See the discussion of sprayers on pages 100–101.

Aniline stains can be dissolved in alcohol, too, as mentioned, and they don't raise the grain. But they dry so quickly that splotching becomes an even greater hazard. Investigate these only if you intend to spray.

Before making a final decision on which staining technique to use, read the next two sections very carefully, especially if you're working with open-grained or coarse-grained woods like oak, walnut, mahogany, or chestnut, as opposed to close or fine-grained woods like maple or cherry.

How do you tell the difference? Run your fingers over a well-sanded piece. The coarse-grained wood will feel very textured, while the fine-grained wood will feel very smooth. Whether you want to finish your open-grained wood so that you take advantage of its texture or you want it to be as smooth as glass, it needs some special staining techniques to get what you want.

USING A PIGMENTED SEALER AS A WOOD STAIN

Penetrating wood sealers or resins come in clear finishes as well as in wood tones, and it's possible to use them as stains as well as finishes. In fact, if you're going to opt for this kind of finish, and your piece needs added color, this is the best way to stain it.

You're going to be hearing lots about penetrating wood sealers in the chapter coming up, but it's worth talking about now so you can make good choices.

Most of the finishes in this book are "surface" finishes. That is, they lie on top of the raw wood, penetrating only slightly. Unless that surface is perfectly smooth, this type of finish will never look right.

Penetrating sealer is not a surface finish. It is rubbed *into* the wood to penetrate its fibers and has little or no shine. The effect is more of an "oiled" look, very like the oiled Danish Modern look so popular a few years back. It also bears a resemblance to the old beloved "rubbed" linseed-oil finish, which generally takes half a year to build up, and an eternity to maintain—if it lasts. (My subtle way of telling you I prefer penetrating sealers, for reasons we'll get into when we talk about finishes.)

The important thing here is that you can use this staining and finishing technique to take advantage of open-grained, beautifully textured wood. No smoothness needed here, or perhaps even wanted in some cases.

Penetrating sealers can look lovely on close-grained woods, too, of course, but with open grains, they also save you the job of applying a paste wood filler.

Clear sealers can be used as a medium if you want to mix your own stain. Thin the sealer with about 25 to 30 percent paint thinner, and add tinting colors to get what you want.

Tinting colors for wood stains are available at most paint stores, and are called by such names as raw umber, burnt umber, sienna (also raw and burnt), Venetian red, ocher, black—in short, the basic colors which can be mixed to give a wood tone. You have to experiment a bit to get what you think is a rich oak or walnut or teak, but here are a few general rule-of-thumb suggestions to get you going. Burnt umber and a touch of Venetian red are mixed to get a mahogany tone. (Caution: a little red goes a long way.) You can use burnt umber with a little raw umber for walnut. Raw umber with a small amount of burnt sienna will give you oak. Here, testing on scrap wood really is a must, and bear in mind that your colors will often look considerably different dry than wet.

Whether you buy them ready-made or mix your own, the agents used to color the sealer are pigments, not dyes, and in most cases, results will be very similar to what you get with pigmented oil or latex-based wiping stains. Colors are not quite so clear or rich as they are with a true penetrating-type dye. However, grain shows through very well, and texture is marvelously emphasized; sealer finishes compare well in beauty to most other stains and finishes.

USING A WOOD FILLER—THE WHYS, WHEN-NOT-TOS, AND HOWS

Again, we're dealing with the problems—or pluses—of open-grained woods, and if you've read the above, and are convinced you don't want a built-up or glossy look marring your texture, you can skip this step. But if, in spite of all, you want your oak or rosewood or teak as smooth as silk and covered with a built-up "piano-type" finish, wood fillers are a must. Without them, no matter how much you sand, you'll never get a smooth, glossy finish.

This may be true even for pieces that were originally treated with wood filler. Mahogany and walnut furniture, for example, often have wood filler applied before the finish is sprayed on, but if you've used a paint remover to strip such a piece down, chances are some of the wood filler was also removed. To get a smooth, new finish, a fresh coat of paste wood filler will have to be applied.

If your piece is to be stained, do it *before* applying the wood filler. Then the wood filler must be tinted to a tone slightly darker than your piece before you start working with it. The reason?

Paste wood fillers come in a "natural" or "neutral" shade about the color of cashew butter—a bit lighter and more creamy than peanut butter. If applied as is to raw wood, any subsequent stain will soak much more into the wood than it will into the filler, leaving lots of light spots and streaks just where you might want them a little bit darker than anyplace else.

One of the advantages of wood filler, aside from its smoothing qualities, is that, if colored, it allows you to darken the pores, giving the wood a much grainier look.

Several manufacturers make paste fillers in wood tones, but most stores stock them only in "neutral." To get what you want, you'll have to add tinting colors, the same pigments we just talked about on page 61. Again, you'll have to experiment a bit, but use the general formulas given for starters.

To simplify mixing, dilute the tinting color with a little solvent first, then mix with the paste wood filler. This will, of course, thin the filler as well, but since you have to thin it anyway, no harm is done.

Before we get to that, here's another way to tint filler to the exact shade you want. Mix it with some of the actual stain you'll be using—but only if you're using an oil-based stain. Use the thickened sediment that settles to the bottom of the stain can after you've poured off some of the liquid on top.

When applying a tinted wood filler, you'll actually be staining the wood as well as filling the pores. The wood simply absorbs the color contained in the solvent. It won't make any noticeable difference on an already-stained piece, but it offers you another staining alternative if you haven't found what you like just yet, and you can tint your wood and fill its pores in one step.

A pigmented wood filler stains lightly and slowly, and its effects on light woods are subtle and beautiful. You can deepen color further if you want by applying it several times, or switching to darker pigments.

Whether you're filling pores, staining, or both, before using the paste wood filler, you have to thin it with turpentine or a similar solvent in order to reduce it to brushing consistency. The manufacturer's directions will usually suggest the amount of thinning required, but as a rule the filler should be about the consistency of a heavy-bodied interior flat wall paint.

Spread the filler on liberally with a brush, covering only a few square feet at a time. Brush across the grain to work it into the pores. Allow it to set for a few minutes until the filler starts to lose its wet look and begins to get slightly dull-looking, then take a folded pad of coarse cloth (burlap is excellent) to wipe off the excess. Rub vigorously with a *circular* motion and turn the cloth frequently as it becomes saturated.

For best results, switch to a second piece of clean cloth and rub hard *across* the grain to remove all excess from the surface before it dries. Finally, finish by wiping parallel to the grain, but this time don't rub hard. You don't want to wipe the filler out of the pores of the wood, just smooth it all down.

Actually, the wiping-off process is the most critical part of the whole operation, so it may take some experimenting before you learn how to do it correctly. If you start wiping too soon, you will rub most of the filler out of the pores, but if you wait too long, the filler will start to harden and become sticky and will be extremely difficult to remove. You may even have to sand it off.

After the entire surface has been filled and wiped, let it dry for at least 24 hours. Then sand lightly with very fine-grit paper. On flat surfaces, use a sanding block that has been faced with felt or sponge rubber.

Paste wood filler must be rubbed off before it gets completely dry. Use circular motion for the first wipe.

On curved surfaces, use fine steel wool instead of sandpaper. Dust thoroughly with a tack rag before going any further.

ONE-STEP COLORING AND FINISHING WITH VARNISH STAIN

It's one of the quickies of the trade, and like most quickies, it has its limitations as well as its genuine uses. It's not something you'd use on your finest pieces, or where you want your great old wood to show through, or on a piece that's going to take a lot of scrutiny. However, if you feel it isn't worth stripping and refinishing the inside of an old cabinet or the inside of a drawer or the bottom of shelves that are not normally seen, but you want a decent, durable, cleanable surface there all the same, varnish stain is the answer.

The very name, varnish stain, suggests that it allows you to stain the wood as you varnish. However, you're dealing with pigments, not wood dyes, and the effect is more like a thinned-down paint or color wash.

Since varnish stain colors and finishes in one step, and can be applied over an old coat of shellac, varnish, or similar finish without stripping, it can be a time and work saver on some jobs. And you can save your time and energy for the finer stuff.

5 · At Last, the Finishes Made Clear—Choosing and Using the See-Throughs

FINISHES CAN DO SO MUCH FOR FURNITURE that it's hard not to wax sentimental over them. They beautify, to an extent that may surprise the novice, and they protect your handiwork from almost all the abuse imaginable. It depends on what finish you choose, but for every function there is a finish, and one for every finisher as well.

In every instance you'll be selecting from two broad categories of finishes—surface coatings and penetrating types. The penetrating finish, which we'll get to shortly, is used mostly on modern and country pieces, where a casual look is wanted, although there are other nuances and imaginative ways to use it. The surface finish, as its name suggests, builds up a protective film that can be either glossy or dull, and is used on fine, fancy, and traditional pieces—what have often been called the pride of the household. Maybe that's why there are so many variations of surface finishes, and so many finishers who prefer them.

The most widely used surface finishes are varnish, shellac, and lacquer. The most popular by far, and perhaps the most useful, are the varnishes.

VARNISHES ARE FOREVER—ALMOST

More has happened to varnishes in the past few decades than to any other finish. Originally made of natural oils and resins, most varnishes on the market today are based on man-made or synthetic resins. Generally, you can use them the same as the old finishes. What's really been added is a toughness and long-lived durability not always available in the old products. Furthermore, they tend to be easier to use—they flow out better—and it takes fewer coats to build them up to a deep and enduring luster.

Most modern varnish formulations have either an alkyd, a phenolic, a vinyl, or a polyurethane base.

Alkyd-based varnish is the least expensive, but not the toughest. Where ironlike wear is not necessary, it could be a money-saver.

Varnishes with a phenolic base work better outdoors than indoors. In most cases, they don't really dry hard enough for indoor use. (Most spar varnishes belong to this category of finish.)

Vinyl-based varnishes are the clearest in color. They dry more quickly and darken the wood less than any other varnish. They aren't as tough as most of the other types, but if clarity, trueness of color, and quick-drying capability are top priority, this is a good choice.

Polyurethane, the newest type of varnish, is the most durable and expensive of all ready-mixed varnishes. Sometimes known as a plastic finish—though it doesn't need to bear any resemblance to plastic—it offers maximum protection on surfaces that take a lot of punishment, such as tabletops, serving bars, and other places where food and liquid spills are common. It can be very useful in bathrooms and children's rooms as well.

The thing to remember about polyurethane is that it dries to an exceptionally hard finish. That means if you are varnishing over an old piece that already has a polyurethane finish, a thorough sanding is required between coats to ensure proper adhesion. If you miss any spots with this sanding, chances are in those areas the bond will be poor and peeling or cracking is likely. If you're varnishing on raw or stained wood—with no finish—the rules are different. With some polyurethane and vinyl formulations, you will note that a second coat must be applied *within* a certain number of hours—usually a lot less time than other varnishes. If you follow those directions, you will eliminate the need for any sanding between coats. But if you wait too long, you will have to sand thoroughly, as above. So read those directions carefully, and you will save lots of time and labor.

Other factors to consider when choosing a varnish are color—or actually lack of color or clarity—and gloss, either high or low.

As mentioned earlier, vinyls are the "clearest," and although all varnishes are labeled "clear," most of them do have a slight amber tone. On a dark wood, it's not likely to make much of a difference, and may even enhance some woods by "aging" and enriching them just a bit. But if it's a light finish you want, or you're trying to retain the original color of the wood as much as possible, then the degree of amber may become important. Ask about how much amber is in the varnish, and test on scraps of the wood you'll be using.

Many varnishes come in either a high-gloss, a semi-gloss, or a completely flat finish. Not each and every finish is available in all three choices, but you can find what you want among the various types available.

If you want a piece to have a built-up, highly polished, piano-type finish, then you'll use a high-gloss finish. But where you want the duller "rubbed" finish, you can choose the rich luster of one of the various semi-gloss or satin-finish varnishes.

Years ago, when all varnishes were glossy, the only way to achieve a less shiny, low-luster finish was to apply many coats of varnish, ultimately rubbing the glossy finish down with powdered pumice, rottenstone, or both. Nowadays, you can get much the same effect—with little or no rubbing, except for smoothness if you're very fussy—by using one of the low-luster varnishes. Your big effort here will be in choosing the right luster for you. Most manufacturers differ in describing the amount of gloss their varnish provides. One company's semi-gloss may be duller or shinier than another company's satin gloss. Ask to see samples, experiment on scraps, buy enough of whatever you choose to finish a piece, and get ready for a "hand-rubbed" finish only an expert will know from the real thing.

Regardless of the type varnish you select, or whether you're going shiny or dull, if you want to achieve professional-looking results you must make sure the surface of your piece is as dust-free as possible. In addition to wiping the wood down carefully with a tack rag (see pages 45–46), try to work in a room that is as free of dust as possible. If you use a vacuum cleaner in that room, wait at least a few hours before varnishing in order to allow the airborne dust (blown around by the vacuum's exhaust) to settle.

As a rule, varnishes are ready for use in the can without need for additional thinning. However, for the first coat on raw wood, you'll generally find it advisable to thin slightly so that it soaks in more and does a better job of sealing the surface. Consult the instructions on the label for the amount of thinning recommended, or experiment with a small amount of the varnish beforehand. Periodic thinning will be required to maintain a consistency that works easily and flows out smoothly.

If the wood has been stained, a thin coat of shellac may be required as a sealer—but here again, check the manufacturer's label to make sure there will be no reaction between your varnish and whatever's underneath. A thin coat of shellac is usually safe to use as a sealer under most varnishes—except for polyurethanes. Most polyurethanes will not bond well over shellac.

Never shake a can of varnish before opening it. It may cause air bubbles in the liquid, which will be difficult to brush out later on. For the same reason, stir gently when adding thinner to varnish.

It's best not to work out of the full can. Pour off what you expect to use in a single session into a separate container and work from this.

Dip the brush into the varnish by no more than one-third its bristle length, and remove excess by tapping the bristle tips lightly against the inside rim of the

When varnishing, never dip brush bristles in by more than about a third of their length, and remove excess varnish by tapping the tips against the rim of the can—never by wiping across the rim. This holds true for enameling as well as varnishing.

can above the level of the liquid. *Never* wipe the brush across the rim. That kind of action is another cause of tiny air bubbles which run back into the can. The thing about those bubbles is that if you get them on the brush, and then onto the piece, they're tough to brush out. If they dry, or even break just as they're drying, it's almost impossible to get a smooth finish.

And now to the subject of brushes and sprayers. When it comes to final finishes—clear and opaque—the brush becomes the most important practical tool. For how to choose, use, and care for them, see "Special Tools for the Finisher" on page 78. You can also use a sprayer to apply varnish quickly and smoothly, if you know how. Frankly, however, it's an expensive tool, and it does take time to learn to spray with skill. If you're going to do a lot of finishing, see "Special Tools for the Opaque Finisher," page 100, in the discussion of opaque finishes, for which the sprayer becomes a more important tool.

Whenever possible, try to work on surfaces that are horizontal. If the piece is small enough (or if you can get a couple of moving-men types to help you with a big piece) turn it on its side or back, and remove as much hardware as you can.

On most pieces, it's best to coat all hard-to-reach places and the least conspicuous areas first. For example, do the backs and legs of a chair, as well as the rungs, before you do the seat and arms. In the case of a cabinet or chest, do the insides of doors before you do the outsides. The idea is to try to work toward yourself so that you are not reaching over or dripping on previously coated areas in order to varnish an unfinished area.

Varnish is applied by "flowing" it on, rather than by "scrubbing" it on. Brush with light, rapid strokes *parallel* to the grain. Then immediately cross-stroke lightly, with just the bristle tips, using long strokes *across* the grain. Follow this by cross-stroking again, *parallel* to the grain. (Cross-stroking simply means

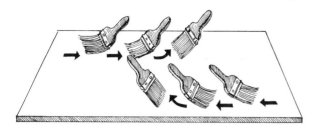

When you can't coat a full length of panel in one stroke, start at one end and go more than halfway, curving up and away from the surface at the halfway point. Next, work the other end and repeat, making sure that the second stroke overlaps the first before the brush again curves up and away.

---

brushing at right angles to the direction from which you just stroked.) For this the bristles should be almost dry, and the tips should be dragged along the entire length of the panel in one single stroke.

Where it is impossible to go from one end of a panel to the other with a single stroke, touch the tips of the bristles to the surface at one end and then drag them about halfway across before curving gently up and away from the surface in an arc. The next stroke is then started at the opposite end of the panel and brought forward until it overlaps the end of the stroke just completed —again in an arc up and away from the surface with a gradual motion. The idea is to never touch the bristles to the surface in the middle of a panel when you're smoothing off, since this will always leave a mark or blemish that will be clearly noticeable.

When varnishing recessed panels or doors that have carvings or moldings around the edges, always coat the molded or carved edges first, then complete the flat area in the center. Dragging the brush across the edges of a piece or a door will cause runs and dripping, so be very cautious in these areas.

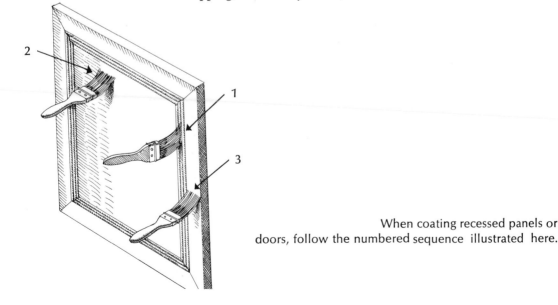

When coating recessed panels or doors, follow the numbered sequence illustrated here.

Although most varnishes specify the minimum drying time required between coats, it's usually best to play it safe and wait a little longer. The only exceptions are some of those polyurethane and vinyl formulations we talked about earlier. Here, the manufacturer specifies that the second coat go on within a predetermined number of hours in order to eliminate sanding while ensuring a permanent bond between coats. Remember, if you wait longer, you'll have a lot of sanding to do.

Except for these special cases, you should sand lightly between coats with 220 or 320 paper. Always sand parallel to the grain, and never sand if the varnish feels the least bit gummy or soft. Use a sanding block to avoid rounding off edges and corners, and sand no more than necessary to dull the gloss and remove any dust specks, air bubbles, or other irregularities in the surface.

On your first or second coat of varnish, you could use a powered orbital sander (see page 27). But all final sanding should be done by hand.

There's another kind of sandpaper we haven't discussed that might come in very handy here. It's silicon carbide paper, generally black in color, with a clothlike, flexible, waterproof backing. Most often referred to as "wet-or-dry" paper, it can be used wet by dipping it into water or light oil. It comes in very fine grades, which are seldom used on raw wood, but it's excellent for sanding between coats. Use it wet for an ultrasmooth final polish, and it can bring a high gloss down to a satin luster.

As a rule, at least three or four coats of varnish are necessary to build up a durable and attractive finish. Use 400 wet-or-dry paper for sanding before the final coat.

Dust is a perennial problem when varnishing, so no matter how careful you are, it is possible that your final coat will show a few dust specks on the surface. If you notice these while the varnish is still wet, the specks can be lifted off by using a finely tapered splinter of wood, or a round wooden toothpick with a pointed end. If you do this carefully and promptly, the wet varnish will flow together to fill in the tiny hollow that remains when the speck is removed.

If you've been super-cautious, and have managed to come through your final coat with no dust or grit on the surface of your piece, you may be finished right now, especially if you've been using a low-luster varnish. If you're very fussy about smoothness, however, or if you want a glossy finish that doesn't have the "wet" look of newly varnished wood, you may be interested in going a bit farther.

Despite precautions, a final surface may sometimes still feel slightly gritty because of very fine dust that settles on the surface as it dries. If desired, you can remove these blemishes by rubbing and polishing the final coat with a powdered pumice mix after it has hardened for several days. This will give a truly professional-looking rubbed finish that will be satiny smooth, and as glossy or as dull as you like.

Though it's basically smoothness you're rubbing for, not luster, you control the gloss by the amount of rubbing and polishing you do, and by the grade of abrasive that you use for the final rubbing.

Start by mixing a creamy paste of powdered pumice (sold in all paint stores) and a lightweight oil such as lemon oil or mineral oil. Fold a piece of felt into a convenient-sized pad, then pick up some of the pumice paste with this and spread it on over the surface. Press down with a moderate amount of pressure and start rubbing with long strokes parallel to the grain where possible. Overlap your strokes by at least half the width of the pad as you work your arm back and forth, but be careful to avoid bearing down hard along the edges or on corners of the piece to keep from cutting through the varnish along these exposed sections.

Pick up the felt pad periodically to add more pumice paste as needed. If the paste shows signs of drying out, sprinkle a little more oil over the surface when necessary to maintain the original creamy consistency. After rubbing for several minutes in one place, examine the surface carefully by shining a light at an angle across a section that has been wiped clean with a separate piece of cloth. As an additional test, feel the surface, stroking lightly with your fingertips. You will know that you have rubbed long enough when the entire surface feels and looks perfectly smooth, and when it has a uniformly dull satin luster after the pumice paste has been wiped off.

At this point some people may prefer to leave their dull luster as is. However, in most cases additional rubbing with a still-finer abrasive—powdered rotten-stone—is usually recommended.

Done properly, a final polishing with rottenstone will restore the gloss that the varnish had originally—either low-luster or high-shine, and in the latter case without that freshly "done," wet look most folks find objectionable.

Mix your rottenstone with oil, the same way you did with the powdered pumice. Now get yourself another clean felt pad, pick up some rottenstone mixture, and start rubbing, again with the grain, just the way you did with the pumice. Remember to periodically wipe a section clean and shine a light across it to determine when you have restored the amount of gloss you want.

If you want to know, by the way, how the shiny piano-type finish was done back then, and still is today, it's very much like the procedure just described, with perhaps a coat or two more of varnish. And so—another mystery of yore revealed.

If you want still more glow or gloss, finish by using a good-quality paste wax. However, if you decide to use wax, allow the varnish to harden for an extra three or four days before rubbing on the first coat of wax. Apply it sparingly and buff vigorously. Remember that a thin, hard coat of wax is more durable and actually provides better protection than a built-up heavy layer.

SHELLAC FOR QUICK AND EASY

Shellac is one of the oldest clear finishes around, and still coats some of the finest antiques, since it predates the invention of what we now call varnish. Actually, it is a kind of varnish, a spirit varnish made of a natural resin which comes from the lac bug, an insect native to India. The original flaky material is dissolved in denatured alcohol to form a sort of deep-orange or amber-brown material commonly known as "orange shellac." "White" or clear shellac is the result of bleaching the material before dissolving it in resin, and it's the stuff most people are familiar with.

Orange shellac can give darker woods a beautiful finish. It's sometimes used on mahogany or walnut to give them an aged look, or to highlight their natural coloring. It's sometimes even used on lighter woods, like knotty pine, to give it an "early American" look.

While white shellac is used most effectively with light woods, you can mix orange and white together to mellow or "age" some of the whiter woods.

Shellac is fast-drying and easy to work with—maybe the easiest of all finishes to apply—and it dries to a beautiful clear wood finish when properly used. As it was once standard for the surfaces of many fine antiques, it's still used to give some of them an "authentic" refinishing job. But it is seldom used as final finish on furniture these days because it does have a number of real disadvantages.

For one thing, shellac discolors very quickly when any liquid is spilled on it—and it's completely dissolved by liquids which contain alcohol. It turns white when subjected to dampness, so unless it's heavily protected with paste wax, it's not a very practical finish on most pieces of furniture.

However, it is still excellent for use on decorative pieces that get very little wear—picture frames, for example, or a beautiful jewelry box—and its quick-drying characteristics can be valuable when something has to be finished in a hurry.

Unlike varnish, unused shellac deteriorates in time, just from aging in the can, so you can't keep quantities of it on hand for more than a few months. Most manufacturers recommend that shellac be stored no longer than about six months.

Some manufacturers date their cans, while others don't, so you are better off buying shellac in small cans only as you need it. If the can is not dated, and you have any reason to doubt its freshness, open the can and look at it. If it's very dark or gummy-looking, don't use it. As a further test, smear a little onto a piece of wood and let it dry. It should get tacky in 5 or 10 minutes and be completely dry in about 30 minutes.

Shellac almost always has to be thinned with denatured alcohol before you can use it on furniture. It is sold in various consistencies, known as "cuts." The most widely sold is 4-pound-cut, although some stores stock 3-pound-cut and 5-pound-cut shellac. The cut refers to the amount of shellac that has been dissolved in a gallon of alcohol. For example, 4-pound-cut means that 4 pounds of flake shellac have been dissolved in 1 gallon of alcohol. To reduce 4-pound-cut shellac to 2-pound-cut, for example, you would simply add 3 quarts of denatured alcohol to a gallon of the 4-pound-cut shellac.

When shellac is used primarily as a sealer under varnish—for example, to keep a stain from "bleeding" through the finish—the shellac should be no heavier than about 1-pound-cut or 2-pound-cut. However, for building up a regular shellac finish, 3-pound-cut is usually preferred, although some experts would rather use 2-pound-cut and apply additional coats. Building up a finish with several thin coats, rather than one or two heavy coats, is how you get the deep clear luster that is characteristic of a fine shellac finish. No other way of application works better.

When building up a shellac finish, sanding lightly between coats and then removing all of the sanding dust with a tack rag is essential for a fine finish. Use progressively finer grits of sandpaper. Start with 120 after the first coat; 220 after the second coat; and 320 or 400 after the third coat. The final coat can be left as is and waxed, or it can be rubbed down with pumice and rottenstone just as you would a varnish finish (see page 71).

Brushes and other tools that have been used in shellac are best cleaned in denatured alcohol, because this is the thinner for shellac (never turpentine or other paint thinners). Or, you can save money by washing a shellac brush with ammonia and water, if the shellac is reasonably fresh.

THE FINE FRENCH FINISH—ANOTHER SECRET OF ANTIQUITY MADE SIMPLE

In the days when shellac was *the* finish for fine furniture, one of the most beautiful—and durable—finishes was achieved by a method known as French polishing. It takes lots of hand rubbing—hours, and sometimes days, of work—but it's also highly practical, since it can withstand years of wear and exposure and can be easily touched up or renewed when necessary.

Of course, craftsmen in bygone days did not have today's modern "miracle" varnishes and sealers available to give them somewhat the same effect without all those hours of work, but some purists still feel that no modern finish can match the luster and beauty of a patiently applied French polish finish. Due to the amount of work involved, few craftsmen today still use this method, but for something precious that you want the fun of turning into something really special, here's how:

1. If the wood has to be stained first, don't use a pigmented or oil-based stain. You must use only a powdered aniline-type dye stain which is mixed with water (see page 57), the only stain over which a French polish will "take." New, fresh, unstained wood is good, too.

2. Pour some 1-pound-cut shellac into a shallow bowl or pan, and fold a clean piece of lint-free cloth into a thick pad. Grasp this with your fingers, then dip the pad into the shellac and start wiping it onto the wood with light rapid strokes, working parallel to the grain if possible.

3. Keep dipping and wiping in this manner until the entire surface is covered, then wait for this first coat to dry hard (usually 15 to 30 minutes).

4. Apply a second coat in the same manner and again wait for this to dry, then sand lightly with very fine sandpaper (400).

5. Remove all sanding dust, then keep on applying additional coats, rubbing each one on quickly and adding coats until you have built up enough of a finish to see a slight sheen over the entire surface.

6. At this point add a few drops of boiled linseed oil to the shellac in the pan and then continue applying more coats by dipping the pad into the oil-and-

---

For a French polish finish, wipe preliminary coats of shellac on with light, rapid strokes. Linseed oil is added after sheen starts to build up.

shellac mixture and rubbing it on. Only this time, use a series of rotary or circular motions instead of rubbing lengthwise.

7. Keep dipping and rubbing, adding a little more linseed oil to the mixture from time to time, until you have built up the depth of finish and the luster or gloss desired. You'll know it when you see it.

You may find as rubbing progresses that you will have to rub harder and more vigorously to keep the pad from sticking to the surface. When this happens add a little more shellac and alcohol to the mixture to keep it from piling up under the pad.

You can quit at any time and resume on the following day if you get tired, but when you do this, it's best to sand lightly before you get started again.

A little experimentation on scrap surfaces will give you an idea of how much oil, shellac, and alcohol you can use, although proportions really are not critical. Experimenting with any new technique, however, is.

LACQUER FOR A FACTORY FINISH

Lacquer has two advantages as a finish: It's very clear, and it's the quickest-drying coating of them all, which makes it very popular with commercial finishers. But most home craftsmen will find it the most difficult of them all to work with. Lacquers dry so fast that they're almost impossible to brush out, which is why the pros almost always spray them on.

Although spraying is much faster than brushing, few home craftsmen have the right type of spraying equipment for use with fast-setting lacquers. In addition, a considerable amount of experience is required to handle this coating properly. It must be sprayed on in many coats, because it forms a thinner film than varnish or shellac, and because of the solvents used in lacquer it cannot be applied over varnish, paint, oil stain, and many other finishes. However, if this is something you really feel you want to try, a sprayer for lacquers is described on page 101.

There are a few lacquers on the market that have been mixed with special slow-drying solvents so that they can be applied by brush. However, these are generally hard to find and offer only the advantage of quicker drying. They still do not give as fine a finish as you can achieve with many of today's quality varnishes.

So why am I bothering to tell you about this finish? Almost all factories use it on mass-produced pieces, even some finer furniture, giving it an importance it may not deserve in the home-finishing world.

PENETRATING SEALERS FOR BARE WOOD FIBERS AND NATURAL BEAUTY

They're the easiest to use, among the toughest-wearing, and one of the most beautiful finishes around, especially if you want a casual, informal look—or one of the new "natural" finishes so popular today. They can even make a period piece go imaginatively with today's way of life, and without losing one iota of its beauty.

They're the penetrating wood sealers, often referred to as "Danish oil" finishes. Made of synthetic resin oils, they're designed to give the type of "oiled" finish which once could only be achieved by repeated rubbing with linseed oil—a finish taking a year to apply, and a lifetime to maintain.

Unlike linseed oil, an organic material, modern penetrating sealers do not oxidize or turn dark in time. Nor are they subject to fungus or mildew growth, also a problem with linseed oil. Best of all, they are far easier to maintain, and a snap to repair—when necessary.

Most important, this is the type of finish meant to take advantage of a wood's texture. No perfectly smooth surface or high luster, no built-up finish; when you touch a piece of furniture finished this way, you know you're feeling wood.

Penetrating finishes gained their greatest popularity on Scandinavian furniture, and are often used on contemporary pieces made of open-grained hardwoods—oak, walnut, teak. What's more, with these woods, you're also eliminating a step needed for the glossier finish—applying paste wood filler. This type of finish is also perfect for today's "country" furniture, pieces beloved for their informal, almost no-finish look.

Unlike varnish and other surface coatings, penetrating sealers can only be applied over raw wood or wood that already has the same type of finish on it—either pigmented stain (page 56) or a pigmented sealer stain (page 61). It soaks into and bonds with the fibers of the wood to actually harden them so the finish is *inside* the wood and leaves no appreciable surface coating or film. Because of this, and because you wipe the excess off as each coat is applied, there is never a problem with brushmarks, and you virtually eliminate the problem of dust settling on the surface to mar the finished appearance.

Because there is no surface film, the finish left by a penetrating sealer has very little gloss. It can be buffed (with very fine steel wool) to a pleasant satin luster, and additional gloss can be obtained by waxing and buffing.

One advantage in not having a glossy coating is that there is no surface finish that can get scratched. The finish is inside the wood. (You can scratch the wood itself, of course.) Most spilled liquids will not harm the finish if wiped up with reasonable promptness, but even if they do, touching up is quite simple. All you have to do is rub additional sealer on with fine steel wool and then buff off the excess.

Penetrating resin sealers come in clear as well as in various wood-tone shades. The colored sealers serve as stains which also help to seal the wood in one application, although you can apply a clear sealer over them. Or you can use a regular wood stain first and then put two or three coats of clear sealer over it. A word of warning, however, on aniline dyes: Color intensifies considerably, sometimes shifting toward a red tone.

Generally speaking, penetrating sealers tend to darken wood more than varnish or shellac, but they will not obscure the grain or change the texture, so in most cases, people do not find the added depth of color objectionable.

You can apply these finishes by brush, or by wiping on with a rag. Application technique is relatively unimportant, since there is no need to worry about brush-marks or lap marks. All you have to do is make sure you apply sealer liberally and work it into the fibers of the wood. The idea is to make certain it penetrates as much as possible—which is why having surfaces horizontal makes the job much easier when this is practical.

Allow the first coat to penetrate for anywhere from 15 to 30 minutes, depending on the manufacturer's recommendations, then use a lint-free cloth to wipe all excess liquid off the surface. Wipe with long parallel strokes, using a moderate amount of pressure, and make sure all excess oil has been removed from the surface before you go any further.

After wiping the surface dry, allow the finish to harden for the recommended number of hours (usually from 4 to 24 hours, depending on the brand), then flow on a second coat and wipe off in the same manner.

Sanding between coats is generally not required, although some experts find that the finish will be smoother and more lustrous if you rub lightly with fine steel wool before the second coat of sealer is applied. This rubbing also helps to open the pores a bit more and thus enhances the penetrating qualities of the second coat.

As a rule, two coats are all that will be required. Tabletops, dresser tops, and other surfaces that can be expected to receive hard wear and more than average abuse deserve a third coat.

After the last coat has dried hard, you can rub on a thin coat of paste wax for added protection. Buff vigorously with a soft cloth to achieve the luster desired.

Waxing is not essential, unless you want some luster and added protection. Just make sure you rub the wax on sparingly and buff vigorously after 10 to 15 minutes.

SPECIAL TOOLS FOR THE FINISHER

PAINTBRUSHES: The paintbrush is the basic tool used in applying most finishes—clear or opaque—so here is everything you'll need to know about your most important helper. You should buy the best brush for the job, and take the best care of it.

Of course, a sprayer could eliminate the need for a brush—*maybe*. And it's true that spraying is much faster than brushing, and a lot easier, particularly when you are dealing with intricate carvings and shapes. For those reasons, we will get to sprayers in the next chapter, on the opaque finishes, where spraying makes a bigger difference. But for the moment, let's say sprayers are generally not practical for the home finisher—not for a clear finish, anyway. For one thing, good-quality spraying equipment is fairly expensive. (Inexpensive units are available, but most of them just cannot do a proper job on furniture.) For another, the technique of handling a spray gun properly takes time and practice to master. Finally, spraying requires a well-ventilated working area, away from the living quarters of the house, where fumes can be safely dissipated (preferably by a fan of some kind).

CHOOSING A BRUSH: As a rule, the brushes most often used in finishing furniture will be from 2 to 3 inches in width. A smaller 1½- or 1-inch wide brush will sometimes come in handy for moldings and narrow strips, and for touch-up work on damaged finishes (see Chapter 7). You'll also want some small pointed artist's watercolor brushes.

Regardless of size, you will want to use only top-quality brushes for applying the various finishes. But you can get by with inexpensive brushes for some jobs. For example, when applying paint remover, an old, badly worn, or inexpensive brush will work just as well. The same thing holds true when applying most stains and some sealers. You usually finish by wiping off the excess with a cloth, so the quality of the brush used is relatively unimportant.

The quality of a paintbrush is determined by several factors: what the bristle is made of, the grade and length of the bristle, and the amount of bristle. Paintbrushes may have either natural bristles or synthetic bristles. The most widely used natural type is hog bristle. The best grades are imported from China. However, for applying fine varnishes and lacquers, many experts prefer badger- or ox-hair brushes. These natural bristles are softer and finer than even the best hog hair, but they do cost far more than the others. You also have to be much more scrupulous about keeping them clean to avoid ruining them.

All good-quality hog bristle has split ends or "flags" at the tip, plus a natural taper that makes them strong and flexible. However, one drawback to Chinese hog bristles is that they tend to swell and lose their springiness when used in latex (water-thinned) paints or finishes. While this is seldom a problem with most furniture finishes, the recent introduction of some synthetic finishes and stains that thin with water can pose a problem if you try to apply these with a hog-bristle brush.

Synthetic brushes may be made of either nylon or polyester filaments, or a combination of the two. Nylon, the first of the synthetic filaments to be used in manufacturing brushes, is still the most popular. It resists wear better than natural bristle, and it is not affected by water-thinned finishing materials the way natural bristle is. However, nylon brushes do tend to get soft and lose springiness when used in hot weather and they get soft and floppy when used in shellac, lacquer, or some of the newer synthetic finishes which have powerful solvents in them.

The newest type of synthetic bristle is polyester, in some ways one of the best all-around paintbrush filaments ever developed. Unlike nylon, polyester does not lose its resiliency when used with lacquer, shellac, and other solvents. Nor does it get soft in hot weather. In addition, like nylon, it is not affected by water-thinned latex paints or other finishes.

Good-quality synthetic-filament brushes use lots of bristles that are flagged or split at the ends, and then tapered by a special manufacturing process so that they closely simulate the excellent working qualities of natural Chinese hog bristle. That is why, when shopping for a paintbrush, one of the first things you should look for is a high percentage of bristles with "split ends" or flagged tips. In addition to a high percentage of flagged tips the brush should have almost all its filaments or bristles tapered so that they come to a fine point naturally. This will enable you to spread the finish on evenly with a minimum of brushing. While a brush with lots of coarse, stubby bristles may be fine for applying paint remover or wood stain (which is then wiped), it is worse than useless when it comes to applying varnish, shellac, lacquer, and other fine finishes.

To check a brush for quality, hold it upside down at eye level. Then spread the bristles out between your fingers while looking through them. You'll be able to spot the tapered bristles and the flagged ends very quickly. If the brush has lots of blunt-end or cut-off bristles which are not tapered and flagged, you'll see them easily.

While you're holding the brush this way, spread the bristles apart and look down into the center of the brush. All brushes have one or two plugs (wood or plastic) to create a partial hollow in the center of the bristles. This enables them to hold more paint and makes them easier to clean. However, if this plug

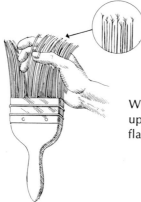

When the bristles of the brush are held up to light, you should see lots of flagged tips that look like split ends.

BLOCK

If the block in the center of the brush is too wide, there will not be enough bristles to hold paint or varnish and flow it out uniformly.

or filler block is too thick it cuts down greatly on the amount of bristles actually contained in the brush. So, when comparing brushes, compare the thickness of these filler blocks. Cheap brushes will have very thick blocks in the center to make them look as though they have many more bristles than they actually have.

A good-quality brush will also be shaped so that its bristles taper to a chisel-like edge. The bristles should feel springy, yet be soft and silky when you stroke the brush over your hand. Another thing to look for in a quality brush is the ferrule or metal band; it should be made of stainless steel, aluminum, or similar rust-resistant metal, and should be well secured with plenty of fasteners to keep it from loosening later on.

You will usually find a better selection of good-quality brushes in a store that professional painters and furniture finishers patronize, rather than in a local hardware store that carries a limited selection.

Brushes also come with handles of different shapes, but this is strictly a matter of preference. Try the different shapes and styles to see which one feels most comfortable. As for size, you'll find that brushes from 2 to 3 inches in width will be adequate for most jobs. As a rule, the less brushing you do, the

In a good brush, the bristles will feel springy and resilient, yet soft and gentle on your hand.

---

better the finish will come out. Use a 3-inch brush on sizable pieces of furniture, and a 2- or 3-inch brush on smaller pieces and on narrower surfaces.

USING BRUSHES: Before using a new brush for the first time, grasp it firmly by the handle and snap it up and down a few times. Then grasp the handle between the palms of your hands and, with the bristles pointing down, twirl it rapidly back and forth. This will spin out any loose bristles and dirt left during the manufacturing process. It's natural for a few bristles to shake loose at this point, but if they continue to fall out for more than a few minutes, the brush has been poorly made and will be nothing but a source of grief when you use it. Return it to your dealer.

There are certain guidelines for brushing worth repeating. Never dip bristles into a can of paint, varnish, or other finish by more than one-third their length. Always remove excess paint by tapping the bristles' tips lightly against the inside rim or sides of the can above the level of the paint or varnish on the inside and don't wipe the brush *across* the rim or edge of the can. This will cause small bubbles to accumulate in the material that runs back into the can, and these tiny air bubbles will be very difficult to brush out when you pick up more material.

Most people find it easier to control the brush if they hold the handle between the thumb and forefinger, much as you would a pencil. Flow the finish on with steady strokes, using only a moderate amount of pressure and lifting the brush gradually at the end of each stroke with a slight arcing motion. This will cause the material to "feather out" and blend in better with the already coated areas as you work from a dry, uncoated area into a previously coated wet section.

Never stop in the middle of a panel or section, and, if possible, start by working across the grain or the shortest dimension of each section. As you complete each panel, smooth out the finish by cross-stroking lightly at right angles to the original direction. (This finishing direction should be parallel to the grain if practical, and should be done with an almost-dry brush.)

As a rule, you'll be able to paint most sections by stroking across from one side to the other. However, if you are working on the inside of a cabinet where it is impossible to let the brush run off the opposite end, or if you are doing panels that are too large to handle as a single unit, then it is best to work from each edge or side in toward the middle. After you have cross-stroked one section, touch the bristle tips to one end of the panel and then drag the brush lightly and quickly across the surface until you are just past the center. Lift the brush gradually up and away from the surface without slowing up your stroke, and then, starting at the opposite end, repeat the process. The two strokes should overlap each other by a slight amount in the center to smooth out all brushmarks and to minimize the likelihood of sags or "curtains" developing later on.

CLEANING AND CARING FOR BRUSHES: There is no better way to ruin a good brush than by failing to clean it properly and promptly after each use. Although many people seem to think of brush cleaning as a time-consuming, messy job, if done properly, it is really very simple and takes only a few minutes.

Some people like to leave a brush soaking in solvent overnight when they intend to resume work on the following morning, but this is not always a good idea. All too often something happens the next day and you don't get back to that job. In the meantime, the solvent dries up, and the brush is ruined. If you do leave a brush soaking overnight, remember that you should never leave it standing in a can or jar where the bristle tips will be resting on the bottom. This will give the bristles a permanent curl, almost impossible to take out. A better alternative is to saturate the bristles with thinner or solvent, then wrap the brush snugly in aluminum foil or plastic, and tie tightly to keep the solvent from evaporating overnight.

If you want to do the job properly, you should clean the brush thoroughly at the end of each day's work, especially if the brush is to be put away for a while. Here is the way to go about it:

(1) Rub as much material out of the brush as possible by wiping it back and forth repeatedly on scrap pieces of cardboard or on a stack of old newspapers. (Tear off the top sheet as soon as it becomes saturated to expose a fresh one.)

(2) Pour about ½ inch of the appropriate thinner or solvent into a coffee can or wide-mouth jar. Then press the brush against the bottom of the container and work the bristles vigorously up and down in the solvent at the bottom of the can to loosen up caked-in material.

(3) Wipe the bristles against the rim of the can to remove the dissolved

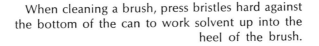

When cleaning a brush, press bristles hard against the bottom of the can to work solvent up into the heel of the brush.

Use a coarse comb to straighten and smooth bristles after cleaning.

paint or varnish, then pour out the liquid and add about the same amount of fresh solvent again.

(4) Repeat the rinsing action by working the bristles vigorously against the bottom of the can, but this time use your fingers if necessary to work the solvent well up into the heel of the brush. Again, wipe the excess out of the brush by drawing it across the rim of the can, then pour this liquid out.

(5) Repeat this rinsing once or twice more, using a small amount of liquid each time. When the solvent seems completely clean and no more material is coming out of the brush, comb the bristles out with a coarse-tooth comb to straighten any tangles. Finish by wrapping with heavy brown paper or aluminum foil as indicated in the drawing on page 84, then store the brush by laying it flat in a dry location.

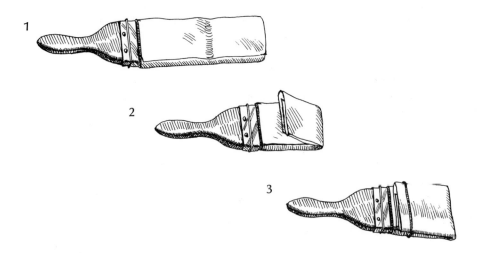

If the brush is to be stored, wrap in heavy brown paper as shown here, and secure with string or a rubber band.

OTHER EQUIPMENT: Special sandpaper, rottenstone, pumice, and other materials used for transparent finishes have been discussed throughout this chapter. As explained, you may have use for a power sander (see page 26) or a sprayer (see page 100).

6 · The Cover-Ups—Working with Opaque Finishes

MAYBE HOME FINISHERS—even the most experienced—have made too much of the opaques as just cover-ups, "easy" ways to hide inferior or otherwise unworthy furniture. The fact is, paints have been used for centuries to beautify as well as protect furniture from plain to fancy to some mighty fine pieces. Chippendale, for example, had a long and successful run with paints, and many good, valuable Colonial pieces, built in the eighteenth and nineteenth centuries, were originally finished this way. And contrary to what many amateurs believe—or what stripping havoc they have wrought—this is the way such pieces should be handled when you refinish them.

True, paints were used back then to cover what were considered the lesser woods, or even a variety of woods that wouldn't have looked attractive showing through a transparent finish—even with staining. But more often than not, craftsmen deliberately used these kinds of woods, with no thought of matching grain or tone, much less species of wood, because they knew they were creating pieces for "fancy" work, as painting was called—which doesn't mean the pieces weren't as well made as any fine piece, or that the wood wasn't sturdy. It's just more practical not to use beautiful wood if you're going to cover it.

All of which does not stop paints—specifically the enamels, the most useful and durable opaques for finishing—from making the inexpensive, less-than-perfect piece look so terrific even its maker would gasp. And there are so many effects you can get with them— from putting them on plain, the time-honored way, to glazing for an antique look, to faking wood, pickling—you'll see as we go along. Whatever technique you use, you'll find that enamel is by far the best way to finish the less expensive and/or poorer-quality woods.

Maybe this is the place to stop and talk a minute about what's meant by "poor quality" or "lesser" or "minor" woods. These labels always mean the same thing. "Poor quality" can mean any wood not up to par—because the tree wasn't healthy or the wood has been cut badly or damaged, etc. It can include a really fine piece with wood so badly scorched, stained, or otherwise marred that only an opaque finish can rejuvenate it, perhaps even bring it back to its former glory.

Pine, hemlock, and other needle-bearing trees are softwoods. They can be damaged more easily than hardwoods, such as maple, oak, mahogany, cherry, and the like. They can still be pretty sturdy, but only hardwoods are considered fine cabinet woods. Hence, softwoods are "lesser" or "minor" woods, and less expensive than cabinet wood, though a fine pine piece can cost more than a mediocre walnut one.

Not all hardwoods are considered fine cabinet woods. Ash, for example, is about as hard a wood as you can find. It's used to make baseball bats. But it has no interesting grain. Fine cabinetmakers often made—and still make—use of this kind of hardwood, and good pine, or a combination of the two or three or more, to put together some marvelous pieces made to be painted. Again, while the woods themselves are relatively "inexpensive," the pieces aren't.

So you see, you can take the opaques as seriously as you like, depending on the piece, and you still won't need to strip, though a nice finish does call for smooth sanding. As for patching, no need to match compound to wood, since you'll be covering your patches, and in one case, at least, you may not even have to do any at all.

WORKING WITH COLORED ENAMELS—FROM SIMPLY BEAUTIFUL TO A FINISH EVEN KIDS CAN'T KILL

While there are lots of tricks you can play with enamel, the most popular way to apply it is plain—for some not-so-plain effects. It's available in a tremendous range of colors, flows out smoothly, has excellent hiding power and spreads easily when applied with a good-quality brush. Two coats will usually take care of even the most extreme color changes.

What makes enamels so tough is that they're formulated with basically the same vehicles as varnishes. In fact, enamels are varnishes, with enough pigments added to make them opaque and give them the desired color. You can get your enamel with an alkyd or a polyurethane base. If your piece is going to take lots of abuse, opt for tough polyurethane. It's one of the hardest finishes around, and wounds are easily patched and touched up.

Many of today's enamels have an acrylic or latex base and can be thinned with water. (Brushes and other painting tools can also be washed in water, which is a big plus.) Generally, however, they do not come in as wide a range of colors as the solvent-thinned alkyds or polyurethane enamels, but otherwise they are applied in exactly the same manner. Some of the newest formulations are practically as tough, but most experts agree that latex-base enamels are not quite as abrasion-resistant as the alkyd or polyurethane enamels are, a minus in the kids' rooms. In addition, there may be a problem with rust showing through if hardware made of iron or steel is coated with a water-thinned enamel. And most do not have quite as high a gloss, if shine is what you want.

Although most people still think that all enamels dry to a high gloss, they actually come in a choice of finishes—high-gloss, semi-gloss and satin. However, since there is no standardization of these definitions from one manufacturer to another, the only way you can be sure of the exact gloss is to see a dried sample of the actual paint, or test it yourself.

Bear in mind that the higher the gloss the more noticeable will be any irregularities or defects in the smoothness of the surface, so if you intend to use a glossy finish, take extra care with the sanding, patching, and filling before any paint is applied.

Gloss also shows dents, knicks, and scrapes more than the duller finishes, so you might want to consider this factor if you're choosing enamel for a child's room. However, kids love the shine—the wetter-looking the better, for most of them.

If you can't find a ready-mixed enamel in the exact color you want, you can start with a color that is close and then doctor this up with tinting colors which you can add yourself. These are like the tinting colors used to get wood tones, but you can only add small amounts without affecting drying qualities. They come in tubes, and you add them slowly to the paint until you get what you want.

However, most well-stocked dealers have paint-mixing systems with hundreds of different-colored chips which they can match exactly by using factory-measured formulas. You can almost always find the color you want via one of these systems. Once you select a color, the dealer can mix it in a matter of minutes, then duplicate it at any time in the future *as long as you have a record of the color number*.

Like any other finish, enamel can be no smoother than the surface over which it is applied, so don't stint on the sanding and smoothing. If you are painting over an old finish, be sure you "feather out" rough edges where the old finish may have chipped off by sanding till smooth. Remove any of the old finish that shows signs of chipping or not adhering firmly, and when finished sanding be sure you remove all dust by wiping carefully with a tack rag (see page 45).

As a rule, to achieve an even gloss and color at least two coats of enamel

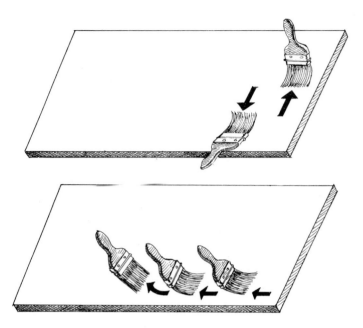

Start brushing enamel on by applying across shortest dimension first (top). Then cross-stroke along length as shown (bottom). Lift brush gradually at the end of the stroke by curving away from the surface without stopping forward motion.

---

will be required. However, if you are applying the enamel over raw wood, or over a badly worn finish, an enamel undercoat will also be needed for the first coat. The two coats of enamel go on after this.

Enamel is supposedly ready for use when the can is opened, but as a practical matter some slight thinning will almost always be required as you work in order to maintain a good working consistency. If you are applying two coats, thin the first coat slightly (5 to 10 percent) and don't try to make it cover completely. The second coat will cover up any "thin" areas that remain.

Brushing techniques for enamel are similar to those used in brushing varnish (see Chapter 5, pages 65–70 and 81–82). Use a good-quality brush with lots of soft bristles (see pages 78–80). With enamels, a good brush and careful technique may be even more important than it is with varnishes. Brushmarks and such are more noticeable in color than they are in a clear finish. A good brush and patience are essential. And there are ways of straightening out some mistakes, as there are with varnishes.

Like varnish, the enamel is flowed on with long strokes and with only a moderate amount of pressure. Never dip the bristles in by more than one-third their length, and whenever possible lay surfaces horizontal to help the finish flow out smoothly.

As a rule, it is best to paint across the narrower dimension of each panel first, then cross-stroke lightly with just the bristle tips to eliminate brushmarks and to smooth out uneven areas. As you work, keep checking for runs, sags, or drips, especially in the corners, and pick these up promptly with the tip of your brush to keep them from growing. However, once the paint starts to get tacky—thick and sticky—you won't be able to smooth out these irregularities, so just let them dry and then sand them out on the following day before the next coat of enamel is applied.

Sanding between coats is not always necessary when using a semi-gloss or low-luster or flat enamel, but it is essential when putting one coat of high-gloss on top of another. Regardless of what the manufacturer's instructions say about drying time, always make sure each coat is completely hard before you try to sand it or start applying the next coat. If in doubt, test with a fingernail—the paint should be hard enough to resist easy indentation.

Then test-sand one spot; the paint should not gum up or rub off the surface as you rub. If it does, the paint is not hard enough for sanding or recoating.

It is possible, by the way, to get the same fine, built-up look with opaques as it is with varnishes. Follow the directions for building up and sanding three to four coats of varnish and rubbing down with pumice and rottenstone (pages 70 – 72), and use either low-luster or high-gloss paint. Obviously, this is hard work, and not meant as a substitute for a fine clear finish on make-do furniture. It is a fine finish, meant for a good piece—a beautifully made campaign chest, for example, designed to be painted, and sensationally handsome when finished this way. You can wax this kind of finish for extra glow and protection.

If you've got a fine, heavily carved piece, originally made of good wood, but now so damaged a transparent finish is out of the question, you might want to consider one of the built-up opaque finishes just described. If you choose your color carefully, and highlight the carving most judiciously with gilt, it could look very rich indeed. Black looks especially well with gilt. Read the antiquing section of this chapter before making a choice. It will give you more ideas about colors to use, as well as another technique which works well this way. Then read about gilding techniques on page 99.

FOR FINISHERS WHO'VE CONSIDERED INVESTING IN A SPRAYER WHEN RELATIVE SMOOTHNESS ISN'T ENOUGH

It's been said that you can't get a perfectly smooth finish by brushing on enamels, particularly the high-gloss variety. Well, there are some good and careful jobs that come mighty close to glass. However, if you have to come even closer—if it's definitely the mirror you insist on rivaling—there's no doubt that a sprayer can give you the smoothest finish possible. But only in the hands of a skilled finisher. Amateurs who've never used a gun will have to do some experimenting to perfect techniques—especially on flat surfaces. (For more about both equipment and techniques, see page 100.)

True, for some jobs—textured or hard-to-reach surfaces such as wicker, rattan, wood that has a great deal of carving, rungs, spindles—a spray gun can be an invaluable tool, even in the hands of an amateur with little experience. But read and experiment anyway, and avoid disappointment.

If the job is a small one, you may not need a gun. Aerosol cans of paint are fine—if you can find the color you want, and if you don't mind the extra expense. The typical 16-ounce can of spray actually has less than half a pint of paint in it, so it's obvious that you're paying a great deal for the container and for the gas used as a propellant. Aerosol paints are much thinner than the paint you normally buy in a can, so you've got to think in terms of multiple coats when using any of these, which can also add to your expense. With a small job, however, it's still cheaper than buying a gun, unless you're going to use it a lot.

In almost every case, standard brushing enamels will have to be thinned if you're going to use them in a sprayer—but the amount of thinning required will vary with the particular brand of enamel, as well as with the type of spray equipment you will be using. If the manufacturer's instructions do not mention thinning proportions for spraying, start by adding about 10 to 15 percent thinner and experiment with this on a scrap surface first. The idea is to thin the paint no more than necessary to make it atomize properly as it comes out of the gun, because excessive thinning will cause the paint to run or drip and will keep it from covering properly.

As with all spraying, whether you're using an aerosol can or a spray gun, it is always best to apply several thin coats rather than one heavy one, and it is important to follow correct spraying techniques (see page 101).

COLORED LACQUERS—PROS FOR PROS, CONS FOR HOME FINISHERS

Colored lacquers dry much faster than enamels, which is why they are almost always applied by spraying. Professionals who have the proper type of spray equipment and are familiar with the techniques involved in working with these fast-drying finishes prefer them for that very reason. They can apply several coats in a single day. However, you have to have a fair amount of experience in order to get a really smooth finish.

You will find information on spray guns and techniques on pages 100–103 if you insist, but aside from its quicker-drying capabilities, lacquer really offers no advantage over enamel. Contrary to what many amateurs seem to think, you can get just as high a gloss with an enamel, and the finish is usually more resistant to chipping and abrasion, because enamels tend to be more resilient and less brittle.

Lacquers also contain powerful solvents which present more of an odor problem when working indoors. More important, perhaps, they generally cannot be applied over old enamel and other finishes, because the solvent in the lacquer will lift or soften the old finish.

Lacquers designed for brushing are available, but they are generally hard to find and the color selection may be very limited. In addition, even though these lacquers have special solvents added to slow the drying, they are still harder than an enamel to brush out smoothly. And they still have all of the disadvantages of spraying lacquers.

HIGH GLOSS WITHOUT A SPRAYER

This is a trick finishers use when they want a kind of built-up shine without going through steps involved in a piano-type finish. It's not quite the same—a lot glassier or wet looking, if you will—but you'll get that shine with less trouble than brushing on enamel, and you won't need a sprayer.

Apply flat paint, in the color of your choice, on your piece. Make it as smooth a coat as possible. Now put a coat of the shiniest, most durable varnish you can find over it. Two coats of varnish will maximize durability.

ANTIQUE OR GLAZED FINISHES—THE CINDERELLA CURE FOR UGLY DUCKLINGS AND DEAD DUCKS

Except for penetrating sealers (see page 76), there is no easier finish to apply. It requires little skill, just some imagination. As for preparation—probably no stripping, and only enough sanding to make your surface smooth. Furthermore, you don't have to patch dents, gouges and bruises, unless you really want to. This finish actually looks good with a few marks. Which could make it a reasonable, even handsome, alternative for a child's room. But not until you've covered it with a coat or two of tough polyurethane, the semi-gloss kind that doesn't need much—or any—sanding.

And for all this, it's an attractive, sometimes even beautiful, finish. It's the perfect way to rejuvenate "junk" furniture which still has some wear in it, and to give character and color to uninteresting pieces. It's also a way of making a great old piece—even some fine furniture, with badly marred wood—sing again.

All this may sound like a hard sell, but, if you like the effect, for some pieces antiquing or glazing may be the only appropriate rejuvenating technique.

Although the terms "glazing" and "antiquing" are often used interchangeably, glazing is actually the process that is used to achieve an antique effect. It consists of a translucent or semi-opaque colored liquid that is applied over a previously painted surface and then partially wiped off. The end result is a two-tone effect in which the top color (the glazing color) partially covers and changes the effect of the base color.

The glazing process can actually be used to create several other finishes where a two-tone, color-on-color effect is desired—such as an imitation wood-grain effect (see page 97) or a "limed" or "pickled" finish. In the last two cases a light-colored glaze is applied over a darker-colored base coat. Glazing, however, is most often associated with the application of an antique finish. And it really is one of the most foolproof finishes an amateur can apply. It requires no skillful techniques—not even special care in brushing on the solid base coat.

Because of the popularity of this type of finish with do-it-yourselfers, many paint and hardware stores stock complete kits which carry everything needed to apply an antique or glazed finish. You'll find a can of semi-gloss base color, a can of glaze coat, an instruction sheet, and sometimes some assorted supplies such as a small paintbrush, a piece of cheesecloth, and possibly even a small piece of sandpaper.

While buying a kit of materials for an antique finish is convenient and often eliminates guesswork as to what the final effect will be (stores display samples of the finish you can expect), these kits do have their limitations. First of all, you will be paying more than you would if you bought the materials separately or mixed your own. Secondly, you will be limited to the colors offered. For example, the kit may show an olive-green background with a dark-brown (burnt umber) glaze, but you may want this same olive-green background with a more grayish (raw umber) glaze, or possibly with a glaze that has more red or maroon in it. Any of these variations, as well as an endless variety of different color combinations, are possible when you assemble or mix your own. Experiment. It's fun.

Applying an antique finish is basically a three-step process:

(1) Paint the surface of your piece with the background color of your choice, and allow this to dry hard. The type of paint most frequently used for this background color—and the one that is easiest to glaze over—is a semi-gloss or satin-finish enamel.

(2) After the base has dried hard, a colored glazing liquid, which you can buy ready-made or which you can mix yourself, is brushed on over the surface and then partially wiped off.

(3) Although not essential on pieces that will get no handling, the finish is then protected with a clear coat of semi-gloss or low-luster varnish. This final coat of clear varnish is often omitted in the prepackaged kits, but it should be applied over any piece of furniture that gets normal to rough handling. Otherwise the glaze coat will start to rub off prematurely. It's easy to reapply, but why bother, when a varnish can make it tough.

The base coat of enamel can be applied by brush, painting pad, or spray. A perfect job is not necessary, but a reasonable amount of care should be exercised to avoid skips, sags, runs, and drip marks. You should sand the old surface a bit to get it reasonably smooth, and remove all wax, grease, and dirt by scrubbing with a detergent, or by wiping down with a paint thinner. One coat will generally be adequate for this base coat, but if a radically different color is being applied—very light over very dark, for example—then you may require a second coat in order to ensure reasonably complete coverage.

Allow the base coat to dry until thoroughly hard, at least 24 hours. Even if the label says it dries in 4 hours, wait longer, because the process of rubbing the glaze on will soften paint that is not completely cured.

You can buy glazing liquid in ready-mixed colors in many paint stores, so if you can find the color you want—and if you don't mind paying a bit more for it—that is probably the simplest method. However, it is not very difficult to mix your own glaze.

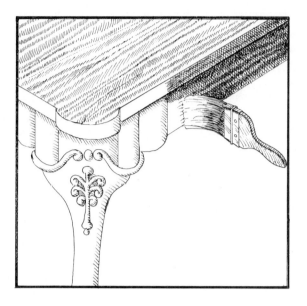

First step in applying an antique finish is painting on a base coat of semi-gloss enamel to act as a background color.

To mix your own you can either buy an untinted glazing liquid which some paint stores carry, or you can use a clear penetrating wood sealer as a glazing-liquid base. In either case you add color by mixing in regular tinting colors, or by adding small amounts of dark-colored enamel in various shades.

Test the shade when intermixing enamels by smearing onto some scrap pieces of cardboard or painted wood first. When you are satisfied with the tone, mix it in with the glazing liquid just as you would the tinting colors.

Since it is very hard to tell beforehand what effect the glazing color will have when it is rubbed on over the background color, some experimentation is essential. One trick that will save time is to paint the base coat onto several pieces of scrap wood while you are painting the actual piece of furniture. These scrap pieces will dry at the same time, so when you're ready to mix your glaze coat you can experiment on these scrap pieces first. This will not only help you decide on the color of the glaze coat, it will also help determine how much you want to wipe off and how hard you want to rub when wiping.

Since the glaze dries slowly, there is plenty of time to fool around with various wiping techniques. In fact, if you don't like the results you can always wipe the glaze off completely with paint thinner and then start all over again.

After the base coat of semi-gloss enamel has dried hard, start brushing the glaze coat on over one section of the furniture at a time. Smear it on liberally, using a brush or cloth, and don't miss any spots.

If you have coated some scrap pieces with the base color as mentioned above, try your glaze on one of these first. Depending on the type of glazing material used, and on the amount of color it contains, you may want to start wiping immediately, or you may find it better to wait a few minutes.

Wiping is most often done with a pad of cheesecloth or a piece of very soft, loose-weave cotton cloth. Experiment with the effects achieved by using the cloth while it's folded, as against using it while wadded into a loose ball. Other effects can be achieved by wiping with steel wool, with crumpled tissue paper, or with a coarse cloth such as burlap. For antique finishes, cheesecloth is by far the most popular method.

The final result is controlled by how much you wipe off and how hard you rub. The more you wipe off, the more the base color will show through, so if your background color is white or off-white, more wiping will result in a lighter overall tone and less wiping will result in a darker tone. By the same token, if

After base coat on piece for "antiquing" has dried thoroughly, a glaze coat is applied and then partially wiped off with cheesecloth. High spots are left lighter than grooves and recessed carvings for a natural, worn effect.

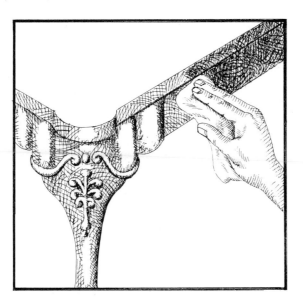

your background color is a dark color and your glaze is a light shade, then the reverse will be true. Bear in mind that the background color should generally be sharper or brighter than you think you will want it to be, because the glaze color will ultimately dull or subdue it to some extent.

The final effect is affected by how you wipe the glaze off. It's probably the most important step in the whole process. The glaze should not be wiped off uniformly. Instead, allow more of the glaze coat to remain in the grooves and in the recesses, while rubbing much more of it off on the high spots. On moldings, wipe parallel to the length of the molding and again remember to wipe off more on the high spots and less in the grooves or recessed areas. In addition, always leave more glaze in the corners where moldings meet.

On flat surfaces such as doors or furniture tops, wipe off more of the glaze in the center of the panel and leave the panel darker around the edges and in the corners. All of this simulates the natural wear that a piece of old furniture would exhibit if the glaze had been worn off over the years.

Again, experiment, this time with wiping techniques, on some scrap pieces. In some cases wiping in a straight line is most appropriate, while in others the glaze will look better if wiped off with a circular or oval motion. Sometimes the most pleasing effect is achieved with little or no wiping and then stippling or patting lightly with cheesecloth.

Each wiping technique gives a different effect. If you don't like the results the first time you try, remember, you can always wipe the glaze off with a rag moistened in paint thinner and then start all over again.

Another process that is often used to enhance the antique effect of a glazed finish is to spatter a little of the concentrated glazing color on after all wiping has been completed. The simplest way to do this is to use an old toothbrush. Dip the brush into the concentrated glazing color, then hold it a few inches away from the surface and flick the bristles with your thumb. This will spatter flecks of the concentrated color onto the freshly glazed surface. You can vary the size of the flecks by varying both the distance between the toothbrush and the surface, and the speed with which you move the brush along.

After the glazing color has dried completely (wait at least 48 hours), apply a clear coat of varnish. Although a gloss varnish is sometimes used, most experts agree that a satin-finish or low-luster varnish is far more appropriate for a finish of this kind.

The varnish can be applied by brush or spray, and one coat is usually sufficient. However, tabletops, children's pieces, and other surfaces that get hard wear will stand up better if two coats are applied. Keeping the surface waxed is also a good idea to protect against spills and staining. If you've got a really nice piece that deserves some attention, or an ornate piece, you might consider giving them a "French" Louis look. For an accent piece, it can work very well.

The traditional base colors for this kind of treatment are white, pale blue, or rich olive green, with a light to dark umber glaze applied over them. Follow painting and glazing directions. A straight wipe is effective. Now turn to "Gilding Techniques," on page 99. The suggestions on page 100 are especially appropriate. Highlight all the carving and frosting, as explained, and glaze with the same glaze you used with your antiquing.

THE FAKE-WOOD FINISHES

Sometimes you will want to refinish a piece of furniture or set of cabinets to make them look like a natural wood grain. The real wood underneath the paint may not be attractive enough to be worth stripping and finishing in the usual manner, or it may be so badly marred and mismatched that a "natural" wood finish is completely impractical. In such cases the same type of glazing process that is used for antiquing can often be used to achieve an imitation wood-grain effect. It's merely a matter of selecting the right glaze for the right background color, and then varying the technique used to wipe off and streak the glaze.

The background color you select as a base coat should be in a beige or brownish tone that is similar to the lightest part of the grain in the wood you want to imitate. For woods such as mahogany or maple, the background should have a slightly more reddish cast, while for oak or pine it might have a creamier tone. Walnut is usually simulated by using a sand color or light brown as a base.

The color of the glazing liquid will have to be quite a bit darker—something like the darkest streaks in the wood grain of the actual species being imitated. For example, you'll want a dark-brown glaze for walnut, while a lighter glaze will be more appropriate for pine or chestnut. For an oak grain the glaze should be more of a grayish or muddy brown. In each case, if you have painted a number of samples with the background color first, you will have pieces on which you can experiment until you achieve the color combination that looks right to you.

Actually, specific tones are not really important in most cases because usually all you want to achieve is the appearance of a wood grain—not necessarily to match a specific type or shade of wood. And as long as you don't place an imitation finish right next to a real piece of wood it's surprising how realistic the effect will be.

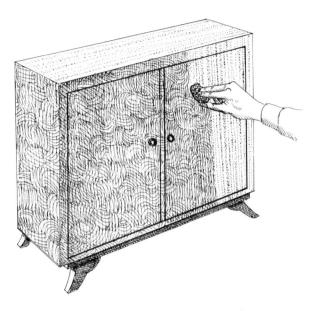

One way to create a wood-grain effect is to wipe the glaze color lightly with steel wool. Then use a dry brush to go over the wiped areas while still wet. Weaving the brush slightly will help heighten the effect.

The most important step, again, is the technique used in wiping off the glaze. The idea is to create streaks that will look like a natural wood grain. One popular method is to first wipe part of the glaze off with a coarse pad of steel wool dragged lightly along the surface. This will create a streaky effect without removing too much of the glaze color. As you finish each panel with the steel wool, go over it again by lightly dragging the tip of a dry paintbrush in the same direction over the same area. This will soften the coarse streaks left by the steel wool and will create a more natural-looking wood-grain effect.

Since no wood grain is ever perfectly straight, imitate a weaving pattern by twisting the brush slightly as you drag it over the surface, and by weaving it slowly from side to side as you move it lengthwise along the panel. Study a piece of natural wood grain to note how it has streaks that weave in and out and try to stroke your dry brush in such a way as to recreate this same appearance.

After you have achieved the effect you want, apply a protective coat of varnish to keep the finish from being rubbed off or damaged. You can use either a high-gloss or semi-gloss varnish for this purpose, but remember that the higher the gloss, the more it will show up irregularities and imperfections in the surface.

GILDING TECHNIQUES

Very often pieces of furniture with carved or molded edges will have these edges finished in gold. It's a technique used on opaque finishes—like the French antique styles—or on ornate wood finishes. The traditional material used for applying a real gold finish is gold leaf, which is not a paint. As its name implies, gold leaf is exactly that—ultra-thin leaves of 22-carat gold metal. These are cemented to the surface with a special tacky varnish (called gold size) that is made for the purpose. The leaves of gold are so thin (four of them are equal to about one-thousandth of an inch in thickness) that they cannot actually be handled with the fingers. They would fall apart. They must be picked up with a special brush by using static electricity to make them cling (you run the brush through your hair to build up a static charge). There is also a type that has a special tissue-paper backing for handling. This permits you to press the gold leaf into place and then peel the tissue paper off.

Gold leaf is extremely expensive, and many dealers no longer stock it. This, plus the fact that it requires considerable skill to use and apply, makes it not very popular with home furniture finishers.

Fortunately, there are a number of synthetic materials which, while not as long-lasting as real gold leaf, will stand up for some time in normal use. Most art-supply stores and many paint stores sell synthetic gold paints that are far superior to the old-fashioned gilt paints used to such garish effect years ago. Better yet, these stores also sell paste-type, wax-base gilt finishes which are rubbed on much as you would shoe polish. These come in a variety of different

Paste-type wax gilt gives a realistic gold-leaf effect in most cases, especially if applied over a base coat of artist's gold-leaf paint.

colors or shades and build up to a beautiful gold luster if they are buffed after they have been rubbed on. You can also leave them as dull and as aged-looking as you like. They are easy to use and often look as real as the real thing.

One good method for achieving a lustrous gold finish is to use a combination of both of these materials. Start by priming the area to be gilded with orange shellac and allow this to dry for an hour or two. Then brush on a coat of artist's-quality gold-leaf paint, using a soft camel's-hair brush. Allow this gold to dry overnight, then highlight the finish by rubbing on a coat of paste-type wax gilt. Spread it on uniformly with a folded pad of cloth, and then buff lightly with a clean piece of cloth. When finished, the gold can be left as is, or it can be "antiqued" by wiping a glaze over the surface as described for antiquing on pages 92–96.

SPECIAL TOOLS FOR THE OPAQUE FINISHER

SPRAYING EQUIPMENT: No one will argue with the fact that spraying is often a lot faster and easier than brushing, particularly when you are dealing with carved moldings or intricately shaped pieces which have many crevices. A good sprayer, skillfully handled by someone who has had enough experience to use it properly, will often do a smoother job than is possible with a brush—but this does not mean that spraying will ensure a smooth, professional-looking finish. In the hands of an unskilled amateur a spray gun can create an awful mess.

Many companies make moderately priced compact compressors and spray guns that are well suited for small projects such as furniture finishing. Light enough to be easily carried around, these generally consist of a compressor which forces air through a hose to the gun. The gun stores the varnish or other material being sprayed in an attached metal cup, and the compressed air coming to the gun from the compressor then forces or siphons the material out of the cup.

To atomize the paint for spraying, the gun's nozzle is designed to mix air with the paint as it is forced out through the nozzle opening. In one type of gun (known as pressure-feed), pressure is built up in the cup to force the paint through the feed tube and out through the nozzle. In the other type of gun (known as siphon-feed), the air comes streaming out through the nozzle past a tube leading up from the cup. This flow of air draws the paint up into the airstream by suction. Siphon-feed guns are used only with lacquers and other finishes that are very thin—they are not suitable for use with heavier-bodied finishes.

The most useful type of spray gun for furniture finishing is the pressure-feed

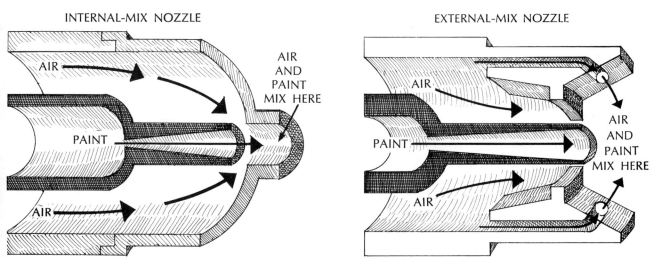

INTERNAL-MIX NOZZLE

EXTERNAL-MIX NOZZLE

Cross-section drawings show the difference between internal-mix and external-mix nozzles on power sprayers.

type. It can handle a wider variety of finishing materials, and it is available with two different types of nozzles: internal-mix and external-mix. An internal-mix nozzle mixes the air and paint together inside the nozzle, then forces the spray out through the nozzle opening. An external-mix nozzle, on the other hand, allows air to flow out through one opening while the finish comes out through another opening. The two streams come together outside the nozzle and are blended into a single uniformly atomized spray. This provides finer atomization than is possible with an internal-mix gun and it is less likely to clog when working with quick-drying finishes that tend to set up inside the nozzle as they come in contact with the airstream.

There is one other type of spray outfit that has become quite popular—the so-called "airless" guns which need no separate compressor. A vibrating motor that is built into the head of the gun atomizes the paint by forcing it out through the nozzle at very high pressure. These units are not really suitable for furniture finishing. They may be fine for spraying fences and other rough work around the outside of the house (the better-quality home-size units can also be used for spraying latex paints on walls), but none of these "airless" spray guns are really of much use in fine furniture finishing.

Spraying techniques: When using a spray gun it is important that you hold it about 6 to 8 inches away from the surface being sprayed, and that you move

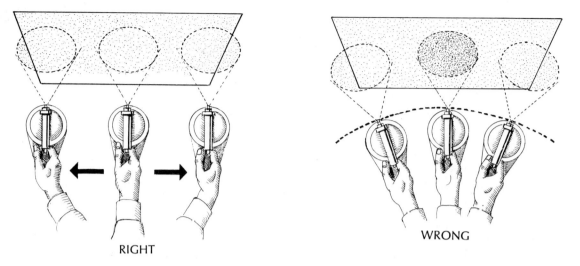

RIGHT

WRONG

When spraying, wrist should be flexed at each end of a stroke so the gun moves parallel to the surface during the entire stroke, and so gun is always aimed straight at surface. Continue slightly past each end before starting the return stroke.

---

it parallel to the surface so that it always remains approximately the same distance away. On flat surfaces, for example, avoid swinging the gun in an arc (a natural tendency). This will bring the gun closer to the surface at the center of the stroke and farther away at the end. In addition, swinging the gun in an arc, with a comparatively straight wrist, also changes the angle of the spray. At the center of the stroke the spray is heading straight at the surface, while at either end it is being sprayed off at an angle. The net result of all this is uneven coverage with possible sagging or running.

Since there are a number of variables that have to be adjusted when using a spray gun, it is important that you experiment on scrap surfaces first. Practice spraying pieces of cardboard, or the inside of an old carton, while you adjust the spray pattern and test for the amount of thinning required.

You will also have to learn how to "trigger" the gun properly. This means beginning each stroke with the nozzle aimed slightly past the end of the surface and then starting the gun moving as you press the trigger. When you get to the end of the stroke, don't release the trigger until the spray is aimed slightly past the opposite side, then release it. As you reverse direction, press down again on the trigger before the spray reaches the actual surface for the reverse stroke. With a little practice you should get the proper "feel" for stroking back and forth in this manner. To keep the gun moving parallel to and equidistant from the surface, you'll have to learn to flex and bend your wrist as you swing your arm back and forth.

Each stroke should overlap the path of the previous one by about 30 to 50 percent. Remember never to stop or start a stroke while the gun is aimed at the work surface with the trigger depressed. Also, when spraying inside cabinets, avoid spraying at a 45-degree angle directly into a corner. Instead, spray the back first, then change direction by 90 degrees and spray one of the adjoining sides. On outside corners it's generally best to spray the corners from a 45-degree angle so that both sides of the corner are coated simultaneously.

On vertical surfaces, start spraying from the top and work your way down.

On horizontal surfaces, such as tabletops, always start spraying the part that is closest to you and then work away from yourself, rather than starting at the far side and working back toward yourself. The reason for this apparent reversal of what seems "natural" is that you are not spraying straight down, so as you stroke back and forth, a certain amount of overspray will drift past the area being coated and settle on the far side. If you were to start at the far side and work toward yourself, the overspray would be settling on already finished areas and would leave a pebbly or "pimpled" finish. If, on the other hand, you start at the near edge and work away from yourself, then the overspray will settle on previously uncoated areas so that it will be promptly covered over as you continue working across and away from yourself.

OTHER EQUIPMENT: You may want to use sandpaper, pumice, and rottenstone as is done for some transparent finishes (see page 71). Brushes are, of course, very important; see the discussion of them beginning on page 78. For high-gloss opaque finishes you should sand between coats and may want to use a power sander (see page 26).

7 · Restoration: When You'd Like It Just the Way It Is, If Only...

WHEN AN OLD PIECE OF VALUED FURNITURE starts to get dull and dingy-looking, or when it accumulates a lot of scratches, watermarks, and other blemishes, most people feel that the only way to restore the piece is to strip it down and refinish it completely

However, in a surprisingly high percentage of cases there is no need for going to this extreme. The piece of furniture can often be rejuvenated by simply repairing the damaged areas and then restoring the original luster to the finish with one of the techniques outlined in this chapter. Nicks and scratches can be patched or covered up, burn marks and water marks can be removed, and dull finishes can be brightened and restored with much less effort than would be required for a complete stripping and refinishing job.

THE NO-STRIP SOLUTION

The first step in any restoration job is cleaning the old surface in order to remove all of the old wax, polish, and oil, as well as the years of grime that may have accumulated on the surface. As a rule, the simplest way to clean wood furniture without damaging the finish is to wipe it down with a rag moistened with paint thinner. Since the thinner is inflammable, work in a well-ventilated room and make sure there are no open flames nearby. Although paint thinner will not harm most furniture finishes, it's best to play safe and try it on an inconspicuous corner or side first to see what effect, if any, this has on the finish.

Assuming that this test shows no harm to the actual finish, proceed with your cleaning job by dipping a folded cloth into the thinner, squeezing out most of the excess, and then rubbing vigorously over a small section at a time. Immediately wipe with a dry cloth to absorb or pick up all dissolved wax, polish, and grime, then continue wiping with thinner. Turn the rag frequently as it becomes soiled and change the thinner in the pan as it becomes very discolored. The idea behind all this is to pick up and remove the softened wax and dirt instead of merely spreading it around on the surface.

After cleaning in this manner, the finish will almost always look dull and may even be slightly cloudy in places. If the finish is otherwise sound with no outstanding blemishes or other defects you may be able to restore it by simply applying one or two coats of a good-quality furniture polish or wax. Try one section as an experiment. Rub the wax or polish on sparingly, and then buff vigorously with a dry cloth. If this restores life to the finish, you can repeat the process on the entire piece.

Sometimes merely repolishing is not enough, because the old finish may be crazed, or so dull that simple polishing will not restore it. In these cases it is sometimes possible to rejuvenate the finish by a process often referred to as reamalgamation. This involves using a solvent to soften up and partially dissolve the old finish so that it flows together and forms a new film that is virtually free of surface blemishes and has a luster that is almost as deep as it was when new. However, to do this you have to know the kind of finish on the furniture. The technique works best with shellac and lacquer finishes; it is seldom effective on varnish finishes. However, most commercially finished furniture is not varnished—unless it was custom-made and finished by hand.

To test for a shellac finish, dip a rag into some denatured alcohol and rub in an inconspicuous corner. If the finish is shellac, the alcohol will soften or dissolve it. If the finish is not shellac, the alcohol will have little or no effect on it (other than perhaps to make it look cloudy or dull-looking).

To test for a lacquer finish, dip a rag in lacquer thinner and then rub one corner as just described above. If the finish is lacquer, the thinner will soften and dissolve it almost immediately. However, lacquer thinner will also break down a varnish finish—but the difference is that on varnish it will cause the finish to blister and wrinkle rather than merely softening it, and it will remove the finish entirely down to the bare wood.

To rejuvenate an old shellac finish with this reamalgamation technique, the simplest method is to rub denatured alcohol over a section at a time. Dip a pad of very fine (4/0) steel wool into the alcohol and wipe this on in straight lines. Allow it to soak for about a minute, then wipe the same area lightly with a cloth that has also been dampened in alcohol. The idea is to soften up the top layer of shellac without actually removing it so that it flows together to form a uniform film.

To use this technique on a lacquer finish that is cracked, checked, or cloudy, the same basic technique is followed, except that you use lacquer thinner instead of denatured alcohol. Some experts prefer to apply the thinner with a brush, rather than with fine steel wool, so experimenting with both techniques may be advisable to see which one works better for you. If you use a brush, spread the thinner on in straight lines parallel to the grain and then wipe immediately with a soft cloth moistened with additional lacquer thinner. Here again, the idea is to do all wiping lightly so that you don't remove the finish—you merely soften it and spread it around so that it flows out to form a fresh film.

After using either of these techniques to restore the finish, let it harden overnight and then build up the luster by using an oil-base furniture polish or a good grade of furniture wax.

RX FOR WATERMARKS

One of the most frequent types of damage to an existing finish is a white ring or spot that is left when a wet glass, dish, or similar container is left standing on the surface. Depending on how long the moisture was allowed to penetrate before it was wiped up, and depending on the shape of the container or spill, the white mark may be in the form of a definite ring, or it may consist merely of a series of spots or "blush marks" on the surface. However, as long as the spots are white, it means that the moisture did not penetrate all the way through the finish into the wood. This means there is a good chance that it can be removed without need for completely stripping off the old finish. If watermarks are dark it means that the moisture has penetrated completely through the finish and into the wood. The only way to correct a condition of this kind is to take off all of the old finish and then sand or bleach the dark marks out (as described in Chapter 3).

If a white watermark on the surface has not penetrated much, it can sometimes be removed by rubbing with a rag that has been moistened with either denatured alcohol, turpentine, or camphorated oil. Try the alcohol first, then the camphorated oil, then the turpentine. If none of these works, then polishing with a very mild abrasive is the next step. Start by rubbing with one of the toothpastes that are advertised as having "extra brighteners" in them—these actually contain a very mild abrasive. Spread a little paste over the white mark and rub with your finger or with a small pad of cloth. If possible, try rubbing parallel to the grain only. If the stain starts to lighten, keep rubbing until you have it all out.

If this fails, try a slightly coarser abrasive. Use some ordinary table salt with a little lemon oil or mineral oil. Sprinkle the salt on first, then dip a cloth into the oil and rub with this. If this seems to be working, then repeat with salt and vinegar, instead of salt and oil. (The vinegar acts as a mild bleach.)

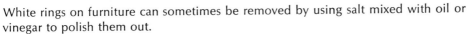

White rings on furniture can sometimes be removed by using salt mixed with oil or vinegar to polish them out.

If the stain still persists, then you'll have to use a paste made by mixing powdered rottenstone with lemon oil or mineral oil. This will remove the stain eventually, although a considerable amount of rubbing may be required. When done, the surface will be quite dull, but you can restore the luster by waxing or polishing in most cases. If much of the old finish has been removed, then a thin coat of varnish or shellac may be required, but try to avoid this, since blending in such a touchup is often quite difficult.

REPAIRING SCRATCHES

Scratches and small nicks that are in the finish and don't go all the way through into the wood can be repaired in one of three ways:

(1) Touch up the scratch with a colored oil stain of the right shade, or with one of the various "scratch-removing" liquids which are widely sold in hardware and houseware stores. This will not fill in or remove the scratch, but it will color or camouflage it so that it becomes scarcely noticeable—particularly after you apply a polish or wax over the touchup.

(2) If the scratch is a shallow one, you can often remove it by using the reamalgamation process (see page 105). A little solvent applied with an artist's pointed brush will cause the finish to dissolve at that point so that it flows together and the scratch becomes scarcely noticeable after it is polished or waxed.

(3) Deeper scratches will have to be filled in and possibly colored in order to completely conceal them. The best material to use for this purpose is stick

To fill defects with a shellac stick, heat the stick with flame until it is soft enough to drip and can be smeared into cavity with a heated knifeblade.

---

shellac. It comes in a range of different wood colors and is made specifically for patching wood finishes. Unfortunately, it is seldom stocked in local paint and hardware stores anymore, but you can buy shellac sticks from dealers that specialize in furniture-finishing supplies, or you can order them from mail-order houses that cater to home craftsmen. You can buy an assortment with enough colors to match any furniture finish in the home, or you can blend two or more colors together to produce the exact shade needed.

To use a shellac stick for patching you'll need an alcohol lamp or similar source of smokeless heat. A cigarette lighter can also be used, but a candle flame is too smoky to be useful. A handy tool to use for applying the shellac is an artist's palette knife, because it has a thin flexible blade that is perfect for smoothing, although special spatulas are also available.

After selecting the shellac stick that most closely matches the color you need, start by heating the blade of the knife until it is quite warm. Hold the end of the shellac stick over the flame until it starts to melt, positioning it in such a way that any molten shellac that drips will fall onto the area to be patched if possible. If this is not practical, then heat the shellac till it starts to soften and scrape some off with the heated knifeblade. Use the warm blade to "butter" the shellac into and over the scratch so as to fill it completely. Actually it's better to build the patch up slightly higher than the surrounding surface and then reheat the knifeblade to scrape off the excess and make it level. If the shellac starts to cool while you're working it, heat the blade again, then stroke it over the hardened shellac to soften it.

Instead of shellac sticks, there are also colored wax sticks which you can buy in most local paint and hardware stores. These wax sticks or pencils (some look like children's crayons, others look like wax-type marking pencils) are also available in a range of colors, and they can also be blended if necessary to achieve a specific shade.

Although the directions furnished usually state that all you need do is rub them back and forth over the scratch until it fills in, a much neater and smoother job will result if you use a heated spatula or knifeblade as described above for working with stick shellac. The heated blade will soften and partially melt the wax so it blends in more smoothly than is possible if you merely rub it on cold. Although wax sticks are easier than shellac sticks to use, wax is not as permanent as shellac, and the repair is not as clear or as lustrous.

After the scratch has been filled in with either one of these methods, touching up with a very thin coat of shellac and then waxing or polishing will help to preserve and further conceal the repair.

REPAIRING BURN MARKS

Small burn marks or scorch marks, such as those caused by cigarettes and hot ashes, can usually be patched or repaired without need for completely refinishing the piece. The success of this treatment will depend to some extent on how large the burn mark is, and on whether or not the scorch mark is only in the finish or goes clear through into the wood itself.

If only the finish has been scorched, you should be able to rub the scorched material away by wrapping a small piece of very fine steel wool around one fingertip and then rubbing carefully with this till all the blackened residue is gone. If the scorch mark is deep and shows some blistering in the center, then

---

Scorched finish can be removed by scraping carefully with the point of a sharp knife held so the blade moves back and forth as shown by arrows.

a more drastic method will be required. Scrape back and forth carefully with a knifeblade held at right angles to the surface. Keep scraping until all of the blackened material has been removed. Then use a clean piece of steel wool to rub the spot smooth. Wipe all the dust away and examine the slight cavity that remains to see if the scraping has gone clear through the finish and down into the wood itself. If a good deal of finish still remains (even though it is dull) then you can probably restore the luster by simply waxing and polishing.

However, if you have scraped most of the finish away down to the bare wood, then you'll want to fill in and build up the slight cavity with several thin coats of varnish or shellac. Apply with a small artist's brush and allow each coat to dry before applying the next one. Use enough coats to build up the finish so that it matches the surrounding area, then polish with 4/0 steel wool that has been dipped into paste wax. Rubbing parallel to the grain will blend the patch in so that it's scarcely noticeable after you buff it.

REMOVING DENTS

Pieces made of softwood may have dents or other slight depressions that can be caused by a falling object or by an accidental blow from a blunt object. When wood is dented, it means the fibers at that point have been severely compressed. In many cases you can restore the wood to its original shape by decompressing or swelling the fibers back to their normal size. The best way to do this is to use moisture and heat to create a mild steaming action. If the wood is unfinished, this is simple—the moisture can penetrate directly to the wood. However, if the wood has varnish, shellac, lacquer, or a similar surface coating,

First step in repairing a dent in wood that has a finish is to prick holes with a pin or small tack.

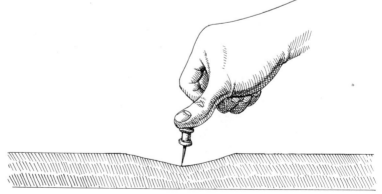

then in order to make this steaming process work you will have to either remove the finish over that spot, or puncture the existing finish with small pinholes which will allow moisture to penetrate. (These tiny holes will be easy to fill with dabs of varnish after the dented area has been repaired.)

Start by placing a wet cloth pad over the dent and then apply heat from a hot iron. The safest way to do this without damaging the surrounding area is to place a metal bottle cap, flat side down, directly over the dent. Press down on top of this with your hot iron. The iron will heat the metal and this will in turn heat the water in the damp cloth under the cap, causing it to steam. This steam will, if all goes well, cause the wood to swell back into its original shape so that the dent is no longer visible.

Place small pad of wet cloth on top of pricked dent, position a metal bottle cap over this, and heat with iron. Steam may raise compressed wood fibers.

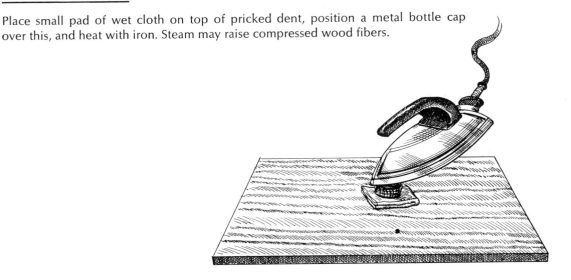

Although this technique is the most effective way of correcting small dents, it is liable to cause white spots or blushing of the finish, because of the heat and moisture. If so, treat these as described on page 106, then restore the luster by waxing or polishing. In some cases you may have to fill in or touch up with several finish coats of clear shellac or varnish before polishing in the usual manner.

HOW TO USE REFINISHING LIQUIDS WITHOUT REFINISHING

Often the entire finish on a fine piece of old furniture is so dull and worn-looking, or so covered with scratches and check marks, that it seems as though the only way to rejuvenate the piece is to completely strip it and then refinish from scratch. However, more often than not if the piece is basically sound and if the finish was originally a good one, then stripping may not be the ideal solution. Besides the fact that it is much more work, stripping may also take away a lot of the original patina of the wood and thus could change its appearance drastically.

When faced with a problem of this kind there is another refinishing method that is often preferable. This calls for the use of a furniture refinishing liquid that is similar to—but not the same as—a regular paint and varnish remover. Made by several companies, and sold through paint, hardware, and houseware stores, these refinishing liquids contain strong solvents that will soften and dissolve most finishes. They remove a surface layer of the finish without taking all of it off down to the bare wood. In other words, the refinishing liquid takes off part of the surface coating and leaves a thin layer of old finish that is reconstituted into a fresh coating.

When dry, it is ready to accept a new coat of clear finish. This method is quicker and easier than complete stripping because it enables you to refinish a piece and restore most of its original color and tone without need for a lot of scraping, sanding, staining, or bleaching.

To use one of these refinishing liquids, you start by pouring a small amount into a shallow metal or glass pan. Dip a pad of very fine steel wool into this and then scrub it on over the surface with a series of circular motions (wear rubber gloves to protect your hands). After you have covered a small area (about 1 square foot), you dip the steel-wool pad back into the liquid and squeeze it several times to flush it out. Then pick up more liquid and repeat the process on the next section.

Continue working in this manner until the entire piece has been scrubbed down, rinsing the steel wool repeatedly in the refinishing liquid. Use a fresh piece of steel wool as soon as the original one starts to shred or show signs of wear. When the liquid in the pan starts to thicken and get very dirty-looking, pour it into another container and add fresh liquid (the dirty liquid does not have to be discarded—you can allow the gummy residue to settle and then pour off the top portion to be saved for reuse).

After each panel or section has been scrubbed in the manner just described, go over it with a fresh pad of very fine steel wool and clean liquid—only this time rub in straight lines parallel to the grain in order to remove all of the swirl marks and circular streaks left by the original scrubbing. When finished, allow the wood to dry for about 30 minutes, then buff lightly with clean, dry steel wool (also very fine) to give the wood its final smoothing.

You're now ready to apply a fresh coat of clear new finish. You can use a

Refinishing liquid is scrubbed on with a pad of very fine steel wool, using circular motions for the first application. The second application is in line with the grain if possible.

regular varnish if you wish, but the most popular material to apply after this process (and the one recommended by the manufacturers of these various finishing liquids) is one or two coats of clear tung-oil-base wood sealer. This penetrating oil is rubbed on with a pad or cloth and allowed to soak on the surface for 15 to 30 minutes. Then the excess is buffed off with a piece of clean dry cloth. A second coat can be applied in the same manner on the following day.

CLEANING MARBLE

Although marble is a beautiful, rich-looking material that is also quite durable, it does need care, because it stains very easily and surprisingly enough is also quite porous. The best way to maintain it is to keep it clean by washing with a mild detergent when necessary, and by promptly wiping up spilled liquids or dropped foodstuffs. In addition, the surface must be kept well waxed at all times with a good paste wax.

When stains do occur and cannot be removed by ordinary washing, then the most effective method for removing those stains is to apply a poultice. This consists of a paste made by mixing powdered whiting or chalk dust (sold in most paint stores) with a solvent which is appropriate for that particular type of stain.

If the stain was caused by a greasy substance, then the poultice should be mixed by adding acetone to the powdered chalk until it forms a thick paste.

Spread this on over the stain in a thick layer, then cover with a piece of plastic food wrap to keep the acetone from evaporating. Use strips of masking tape around the edges to hold the plastic down.

Allow this to remain in place overnight, then remove the poultice and rub the stained area vigorously with a dry cloth. Repeat if the stain has not been completely removed.

Stains that are caused by spilled beverages such as tea, coffee, soft drinks, fruit juices, and most other organic materials such as tobacco or flowers can also be removed with a poultice, but in this case you'll have to use a bleaching solution instead of a solvent. The most effective one is hydrogen peroxide hair bleach, which you can buy in most drugstores. Mix this with the whiting to form a thick paste and spread it on over the stain. Add a few drops of household ammonia to start the chemical reaction, then cover immediately with plastic. Allow to remain overnight and then rub with a dry cloth to see if the stain has lightened considerably. If so, repeat once or twice as necessary. If the stain doesn't lighten very much after the first application, try a poultice with straight household ammonia to see if this is more effective.

The most difficult kind of stain to remove from marble is a rust stain—usually caused by allowing something metal to remain on the surface for some time while moisture is present. If this stain is relatively fresh and has not penetrated too deeply, you may be able to remove it by simply rubbing hard with a coarse, dry cloth. If the stain doesn't come off, then you'll have to try a poultice. Mix a liquid rust remover (sold in hardware stores) with the powdered whiting and allow to stand for several hours to see if this draws the stain out. Sometimes using a rust-remover poultice first, then following with another poultice containing a bleach, will do the trick where simple treatment with rust remover alone fails to remove the entire stain.

POLISHING MARBLE

Many of the liquids and other substances that stain marble will also eat their way into and slightly etch the surface of the marble, leaving it dull or rough-looking. Also, after a poultice has been used to remove a stain the area will sometimes come out dull or unfinished-looking and in need of polishing. For this a special polishing powder called tin oxide is used. You can buy it from many local marble dealers, and it is included in the kits that some department stores sell for cleaning and polishing marble.

To do the polishing job you first wet the surface of the marble with water,

Most marble stains can be removed by applying a poultice made of powdered chalk and solvent or bleach (left). Cover mixture with plastic wrap to keep it wet overnight (right).

then sprinkle the powder liberally over the area. Fold a piece of cloth into a thick pad and then rub vigorously with this until the etch mark disappears and the surface luster is restored. Portable electric buffers can be used to speed the task if the entire surface must be polished, since a considerable amount of rubbing is required to do the job properly.

In extreme cases where home removal techniques fail, or where considerable polishing is required, it may be more practical to remove the marble top and bring it to a professional marble dealer for polishing. He has the machines and materials needed to do this kind of work properly. Just remember that whether you do the job yourself or have it done professionally, the marble must be kept waxed with a good-quality white paste wax if you want to keep stains from causing additional problems in the future.

8 · Buying It in the Raw—Special Pointers on Unfinished Furniture

BY AND LARGE, the finishing techniques described throughout this book apply to all kinds of furniture. However, so many people are buying unfinished furniture as a moderately priced alternative to the very high cost of even ordinary finished furniture—never mind special or quality merchandise—that a special section, devoted to the specific problems of buying and finishing these pieces, seems in order.

Today, unfinished furniture comes in an enormous range of styles and sizes, and varies greatly in quality. Some pieces are surprisingly well made of moderate to good grades of wood, while others are poorly constructed of inferior grades of lumber that have not even been properly sanded. Softwoods are most often used, particularly pine, but even in some poorly stocked neighborhood stores better pieces in hardwood are making an appearance. What's more, there are many alternatives to the neighborhood store. It's true that most dealers stock primarily mass-produced pieces in standard styles and sizes—but there's a whole lot more out there you ought to at least know about. In fact, some unfinished furniture climbs out of the inexpensive or even moderately priced category. Some of it is pretty expensive!

WHAT'S AVAILABLE—FROM MUSEUM-QUALITY REPRODUCTIONS TO PLAIN PINE AND PLYWOOD

A growing category of unfinished furniture available to the public at large is the stuff dreams are made of—home finishers' dreams, at any rate. These are the "museum-quality" reproductions you finish yourself. Many of the pieces are marketed by museums devoted to the preservation of the great American styles—the Henry Ford Museum in Dearborn, Michigan, for example, or the Shelbourne Museum of Massachusetts. You can get American Queen Anne, Colonial country, Federal, Shaker—and all in the appropriate woods, mahogany, walnut, cherry, pine, etc. Suggestions for finishing, or sometimes a kit, come with the package.

The thing that keeps this type of unfinished furniture in the dream category for many is price. It's expensive. Pieces also may come unassembled, to be put together by you—if you want to. Although you often have to order, sight unseen, by mail, in all fairness the museum-merchandised pieces do have a reputation for being of genuinely good quality, with beautiful dovetailing, pegging, etc.

Some fine-furniture stores also sell very good quality unfinished furniture—finely cut, good woods, terrific styles. They also tend to be expensive, but not always.

There are also some reasonably priced, well-styled and well-made pine pieces at a number of furniture marts and department stores which bear no resemblance to the cheaper pine pieces you've seen at conventional unfinished-furniture shops.

Local unfinished furniture stores vary from neighborhood to neighborhood. Some are very good, with decent, well-cut reproductions of their own—reasonably stylish Chippendale, for example, as well as French and Italian country, early American Windsor chairs, and some very handsome modern adaptations of the same.

Some stores which don't carry such a variety, or confine their woods to pine, poplar, birch, and gumwood, will custom-make pieces of oak and other hardwoods at a fairly reasonable cost.

Unfortunately, however, too many neighborhood stores carry only the mass-produced, unimaginative, not-very-well-made pieces in hardboard or flakeboard. But if price, style, and strength are right, you can add the imagination when you finish these pieces.

No matter what the price range, all unfinished furniture has problems, but you can make those problems work for you, especially in the less expensive, more widely available pieces.

WHAT TO LOOK FOR

When shopping for unfinished furniture, it's always a good idea to examine the actual piece that you will be taking home (or having delivered), not just a floor sample or model. Unfortunately, quality can vary considerably, even from the same manufacturer, and some dealers have been known to display samples that are much more smoothly sanded and carefully assembled than the pieces that the customer actually receives.

Look for splits, cracks, dents, and other defects that will need repair or patching—particularly if you're not going to use an opaque paint or enamel. Examine the sides, back, and undersides, as well as the front and top. If the piece has doors, open these wide and examine the backs of the doors and the insides of the cabinet as well as the outside.

If the piece is a dresser or chest, remove the drawers so that you can examine the construction on the inside. See if drawer slides are solidly mounted and smooth enough to permit easy opening and closing, and examine the drawers themselves, to see if they are constructed with solid joints that will not loosen easily when the drawer is fully loaded.

Don't expect to find the kind of dovetailed interlocking joints that you'll find on well-made high-priced furniture—unless you're looking at high-priced furniture—but there should be more than just two or three nails holding the whole drawer together. Also, the bottom of the drawer should be strong enough to carry the load it will normally contain without getting pushed out through the bottom.

Also, make sure corners meet, and are not coming apart on cabinets and chests. If you like the chair but the wood or whatever looks odd, and you think you might take a chance on finishing with an opaque paint if it's strong, sit on it—harder than you normally would.

Lean on tables, ask what the parts taking the strain are made of—the legs, rungs, and spokes of certain chairs, for example. Also, look at the wood with the type of finish you have in mind. Do you want to cover it, or let it show through?

If you're planning a clear finish, with or without stain, you'll want wood free of blemishes, with all the parts matching in color, tone, and grain pattern. Remember that smooth white grainless pine, even a good grade, might not look interesting stained or varnished. But with good pine, there are special ways, you'll see.

If you're shopping for children's furniture, or for some similarly heavy-duty piece, you'll want to remember that pine is a soft wood, and unless the piece is bulky, it might not withstand hard wear. Such pieces have been known to crack and splinter.

On some pieces, it's the strength of the wood rather than the beauty of it that might be important. That Chippendale we talked about, for example. If it's a chair, it ought to be strong, but it's a style that's all wrong for stain and/or varnish. It was always enameled, and looks good antiqued, and the appearance of the wood is the least of your problems.

The same is true for some plywoods and compositions. They can be pretty junky-looking but they are strong, and if they're well cut and attractive and the price is right, a good opaque finish might carry the day until the real thing comes along.

If you see a piece you love, by the way, that's heavily carved but a bit short on grain, and you want a transparent finish, chances are the carving will make up for the absence of grain. On the other hand, lots of French and Italian pieces were painted, as were early Windsor chairs.

By now, you ought to know what the finishes are—if you don't, we'll remind you—but with unfinished furniture, there are bound to be some problems preparing for the finish.

PREFINISHING PROBLEMS

Although the furniture will have been sanded relatively smooth by the manufacturer, nine times out of ten additional sanding will be required before you finish it. For this, hand sanding is recommended—unless the manufacturer's job was extremely poor. Use 220 sandpaper with a sanding block for flat surfaces, and use fine steel wool on curved surfaces and on round spokes or spindles. Rather than trusting to a visual examination, determine smoothness by feeling the surface with your fingertips. Stroke lightly in different directions until you feel the wood is perfectly smooth and all the "fuzziness" that is characteristic of much unfinished furniture is gone. When finished, remove all dust by using a tack cloth (see page 45).

Although nails, screws, and other hardware used to join pieces together are never visible in good-quality furniture, this is not necessarily true when you buy some unpainted furniture—particularly the lower-priced, mass-produced versions. If nails or screws are visible, they should be countersunk (recessed) so that you can hide the nail heads by covering with a wood putty or wood plastic.

To countersink nails, use a nailset and a hammer to drive the heads down slightly below the surface of the wood. However, where screw heads are visible, remove the screws completely, then use a counterbore or drill that is the same diameter as the screw head. Drill a shallow hole just deep enough to permit recessing the screw's head below the surface, being careful to go no deeper than necessary. Then replace the screw.

For filling the nail holes or screw holes that are left after the heads have been recessed, you can use a powdered wood putty or one of the plastic patching compounds which are widely sold for this purpose in all paint and hardware stores. However, if you plan to apply a wood stain to the piece, let this filling operation go until *after* the stain has been applied—otherwise each filled hole will stand out noticeably, because a wood stain will not soak into the patching compound the same way as it does into the wood itself (see pages 41–42).

Once we start talking about staining, you know it's time to make finishing decisions again. You'll again be looking at your wood and deciding if it warrants a transparent or near-transparent finish—that is, just plain varnish, or staining with varnish over it, or a penetrating resin sealer which can be used clear or with pigment for one-step staining and finishing. There is also a special finish for pine that's very exciting—a cross between transparent and opaque, but not quite translucent. It could change the way you look at or treat pine forever. And, of course, the most popular way to treat inexpensive unfinished furniture is with a paint or enamel that completely covers the piece with color.

SPECIAL EFFECTS—THE "SCRUBBED" LOOK JUST FOR UNFINISHED PINE

So many denigrating things have been said about pine—and so many bad things have been done to it. It's always masquerading as some fancier wood, and we're always being warned that it doesn't quite cut it anyway—so maybe we ought to cover it entirely with paint. How refreshing then to find a finish which lets pine be pine—and so beautifully. And it's absolutely right with decent-quality brand-new, unfinished pine.

Sometimes called "scrubbed pine," it's one of the more popular kitchen finishes in Europe, but the technique was popular here years ago. It was sometimes called "pickled pine" or "blond" when used primarily as a lightening technique, or "limed oak" when a light gray stain was used first (to simulate oak) or when actual oak was used. It is still popular among finishers who know about it. The look you're aiming for here is rather like old pine (don't use old pine; it's too precious and you can use that "mellow" look someplace else) that's been white-washed and then scrubbed, so that the paint looks as though it's penetrated part of the wood, with lots of bare wood still showing through.

A word of caution when you're choosing a pine piece to use this way. Look for a better grade of pine with some grain. As mentioned, much of today's unfinished pine furniture is so devoid of grain that using this technique might leave you with a bland, characterless finish. So shop for your piece carefully; you can find some decent pine even in cheap unfinished furniture shops.

Before you begin, all cavities need to be filled. Pay special attention to dents and unevenness around knots and use wood putty or compound to smooth them over. Keep it light, like the wood, but there's no need for an exact match, because you'll be obscuring much of it. Get it as smooth as you can, with a light finishing sanding.

Now seal the wood with a thin "wash" of shellac.

The formula is the same for any soft wood on which stain might not take evenly—1 part ordinary white shellac to 2 parts denatured alcohol. This will help smooth out the wood, and allow the paint you're going to use to wipe over the wood more uniformly. Keep the coat you put on thin. Brush on with a wide brush to avoid overlapping any more than necessary, so the paint can penetrate somewhat.

Allow the shellac to dry for about an hour, then sand lightly with fine-grit (220) sandpaper to take down the slight fuzz that will be left by raised grain after the application of the wash-coat shellac. Remove any dust with a tack rag.

Now brush on an ivory-colored, oil-base flat paint—and then quickly wipe off with a folded pad of cloth. Wipe with the grain until you've got as much paint off with as much wood as you want showing.

Remember to do a small section at a time, or else the paint will dry before you can wipe, and you'll be left with a stripping job.

Let your piece dry overnight. Once it's completely dry, cover your "scrubbed" finish with two coats of low-luster polyurethane. Polyurethane is absolutely the best varnish for softwoods, which are particularly subject to expansion and contraction with changes in humidity; the varnish you use on them should be one that will "give" without cracking. One of the toughest and most flexible varnishes you can use is polyurethane.

For more about varnishing, see page 65.

SPECIAL STAINING AND FINISHING TECHNIQUES

If you've discovered a really beautiful piece of unfinished furniture, well made of a blemish-free, beautiful wood, you've got no problem. Any finish in this book will do. In fact, if you've indulged yourself in one of those "museum-quality" pieces, you might want to try the French polish finish, on page 73, which works perfectly on raw wood. (If you're going to stain, and want to use this finish, remember that you must use aniline or water-base dyes.) This might be just the moment to take advantage of that finish. With any other finish, experiment a bit in some obscure spot. Even hardwood, when it's raw, can be a bit porous.

But if you've gone to a neighborhood emporium and paid a modest price, softwood is probably what you've got. Bear in mind that some of the softwoods used in making unfinished furniture do not always take a stain uniformly, which means you may have to partially seal the wood, the way we described on page 55. Experiment first on the back or underside of your piece, where the tests won't show.

If your test indicates that the stain does not take evenly—that is, it comes out blotchy or uneven, or it soaks in so fast that you don't have time to wipe it off uniformly—then you should partially seal the surface of the wood before you apply the stain. The simplest way, as mentioned, is to brush on a thin coat of clear, white shellac diluted with about 2 parts denatured alcohol. This will partially seal the surface of the wood, yet it will still allow the stain to "take" satisfactorily. Again, use a wide brush to avoid overlapping. Allow to dry for about an hour. Then rub down lightly with very fine sandpaper or steel wool to take off the fuzz.

Again, the warning: If you're staining a softwood to look like a hardwood, you may not get the same colors on your wood as the stain samples displayed by the dealer, or the color card supplied by the manufacturer. Remember, don't expect any stain to make a piece of pine look like walnut or mahogany (even if the color has that name)—just try to select a pleasing tone that will blend well with the furnishings in that room. A stain will only change the color of the wood—not its grain pattern or texture.

A piece of pine can look very handsome as just a piece of pine. Antique pine, for example, is quite beautiful. It's a kind of reddish brown that seems to have fiery highlights with a finish over it. It's almost impossible to duplicate exactly, but experiment with a stain that's a cross between a light walnut and a brown mahogany. You might like the results very much. (Do your experimenting on lumber scraps, but remember, there are many qualities of pine.)

If you don't like the "fake" aging, try this for a mellow-looking pine—cover it with orange shellac. If your wood comes up too orange, cut it with a little white shellac for a more yellow look. Somewhere between the two is what some finishers call "pumpkin pine." This works best, of course, on clear or blemish-free pine. Finish with a couple of coats of good varnish, but make sure the varnish you select can be used over shellac (some can't).

If you're going to stain, you will generally be better off with one of the pigmented wiping stains, rather than with a penetrating stain. The creamy, semi-paste stains, many of which are latex-base, work particularly well on furniture of this kind.

The stain can be applied with a rag or a brush. It should be spread on evenly and then wiped down with clean rags within five minutes. The wiping removes excess stain and creates a uniform shading that minimizes differences between darker and lighter tones. Allow the stain to dry overnight, then proceed with the application of the first coat of varnish. You can use either a high-gloss or a semi-gloss varnish, but be prepared to apply at least three coats if you want a smooth-looking, built-up finish that will have some depth and durability.

Flow each coat of varnish on liberally, using a good-quality brush, and be sure you cross-stroke each panel carefully to even out brush strokes and eliminate the likelihood of sags or drips. Most polyurethane varnishes do not require sanding between coats—as long as you apply the second coat within a specified time—but with other varnishes sanding between coats will be required. You must not skip or miss any spots; if you do the new coat will not bond properly and may peel or flake.

A PENETRATING SEALER FINISH

A resin-type penetrating sealer which gives wood furniture a "Danish oil" or rubbed effect is particularly suitable for unfinished furniture, which tends to be largely informal. Many feel this is more pleasing than a built-up varnish finish, especially on the plain modern or country pieces. It is also a lot easier to apply. You can wipe the resin sealer on with a rag, brush, or painting pad, since there is no need to worry about brushmarks or sags in the finish, and on horizontal surfaces you can even pour a pool of the sealer onto the wood and then simply spread it around with a cloth.

Penetrating sealers are designed to soak into the pores of the wood and leave little or no surface coating. After you mop on each coat, wait a few minutes for it to soak in, then wipe off all excess with clean cloths. The idea is to leave little or no surface coating on the wood. It should all be done inside the pores. As a practical matter, however, the finish will build up to some extent so that you'll get a pleasantly lustrous coating that does have some depth to it. Anywhere from two to four coats will be required on most woods, after which a light coat of paste wax is advisable on surfaces that get hard wear.

Most penetrating sealers come in clear, as well as in a number of popular wood tones (walnut, oak, mahogany, etc.). The clear sealers will darken raw wood slightly—more than a varnish will—giving it a sort of amber or golden cast that enhances its natural appearance. The pigmented sealers, on the other hand, act as both a stain and a finish.

Drying time varies from 4 to 24 hours between coats, and as a rule no sanding is required between coats. However, if the surface feels slightly fuzzy after each coat dries, then a light rubdown with fine steel wool or very fine sandpaper before the next coat is applied will help ensure a smoother overall finish.

SPECIAL PAINTING TECHNIQUES

Colored enamels in either a high-gloss or satin finish are often used on unpainted furniture, because this is the quickest and easiest way to cover up otherwise drab-looking or unattractive woods as well as to brighten up interior furnishings. Enamels must be preceded by a base coat of enamel undercoat (also called enamel underbody) when applied to raw wood. Thin this with the appropriate solvent to facilitate easy spreading and better penetration, and brush it on as carefully as though it were the finish coat.

Before starting, remove all drawers from chests or dressers and take doors off where possible. Lay pieces horizontal for maximum ease of brushing and for the smoothest possible results (the paint flows out better on a horizontal surface).

Available only in white, enamel undercoats can be tinted to pale or medium shades in order to facilitate covering with dark colors later on. Use tinting colors sold in all paint and hardware stores, but don't attempt to tint the undercoat to a really dark shade, since this can weaken the paint and may interfere with its drying qualities.

After the undercoat has dried hard, sand lightly with fine-grit paper (220), then dust thoroughly. If any spots seem porous or not completely covered, apply a second thin coat of the same undercoat before going ahead with the enamel.

When the second coat has dried, sand it until it feels smooth, then remove all dust by wiping carefully with a tack rag.

Now you're ready for your first coat of enamel in the color of your choice. Thin this coat by about 10 percent with the solvent recommended for that particular product. Don't make the mistake of trying to cover completely with this first coat. You'll need at least two coats for a good job, and you may want a third coat in some cases.

In addition to solid-color enamels, you can also apply one of the antique or glazed finishes if you would like to give the piece a softer look or a slightly two-toned effect. You can also soften the effect of a very bright color by rubbing a glaze on after the last coat has dried hard, but this only works satisfactorily when done over a satin-finish or semi-gloss enamel—not over a high-gloss. Detailed instructions for mixing and applying the glaze colors, and for achieving an antique type finish, are given in Chapter 6.

DETAILS FOR UPGRADING

If the piece has drawers, it is a good idea to shellac the insides and backs of the drawers at the same time that you finish the rest of the piece. Although these parts do not normally show, shellacking them will keep the wood from absorbing moisture and swelling or warping in the future. It will also help keep the drawers working smoothly. One thin coat of shellac (4-pound-cut thinned half-and-half with alcohol) is all that is required to protect the wood from warping or buckling. It will also make it easier to keep the insides of the drawers clean.

Because unfinished furniture is made and sold with an eye to keeping prices down, it often has inexpensive and/or very plain-looking hardware (knobs, pulls, etc.). It may pay to remove and discard this hardware and replace it with something that is richer and more attractive. It is amazing how a dramatic change can be brought about by simply replacing a few pieces of hardware on a simple boxlike dresser or chest—after you have applied an attractive finish, of course. And some really handsome hardware is available.

There are so many ways to make even the plainest, least expensive piece take on a new life. Throughout this book, ideas for face-lifting and protecting furniture abound. Use the techniques on unfinished furniture, and on old pieces that are inexpensive as well as those that are valuable. I think you'll wind up enjoying the finishing as much as the finished product!

INDEX